Healing & Recovery

Perspective for Young Men with Sexualized Attachments

Floyd Godfrey, PhD

Editors:
John McLean
Cori J. Gillespie

Healing & Recovery
Perspective for Young Men with Sexualized Attachments

Copyright © 2022 by Floyd Godfrey, PhD., Healing & Recovery, LLC All Rights Reserved

Edited by Cori J. Gillespie and John McLean

ISBN - 9780578904825

Printed in the United States of America

Publisher: Healing & Recovery, LLC

Cover Photography by Cody & Calli Carlson, Abide Studios

Endorsements

"Healing and Recovery will become the 'go-to book' for those reaching out the hand of help to young boys and men seeking to understand their struggle. It safely skirts the political pressures and moves into the heart of the problem - who am I? Researched, documented and supported by science it offers sound direction for one choosing recovery. Thank you, Floyd, for this healing, hope-filled gift."

Mary Anne Fifield, DMFT, CAS-R, CSAT, LMFT
Founding Director of the Addiction Recovery Center

"Finally! A much-needed book for teen males who are dealing with confusion and shame around their sexuality. Godfrey's vulnerable sharing of his personal experiences connects with teens authentically and normalizes this common struggle. He bypasses the typical religious "solutions" and provides sound information about how legitimate needs become sexualized. This exploration of attachment wounds and how to heal them should be the go-to book for every clinician and pastor who wants to truly help teens who struggle with sexuality."

Marnie C. Ferree, LMFT, CSAT
Founder & Director, Bethesda Workshops

"Dr. Godfrey provides an intimate and candid look into what is essential when treating problematic sexual behaviors in adolescent young men. This workbook will serve as the core curriculum of many adolescent treatment programs around the country."

Dr. Matthew Hedelius, Psy. D., LCSW, CSAT-S
Founding Director of Paradise Creek Recovery Center

"A very personal book that is both candid and insightful as to the inner struggles of youth who are dealing with attachment wounds and unmet emotional needs that have been eroticized. It is also a workbook that provides a practical step-by-step process for recovery--which will be helpful not only to the individuals struggling with sexualized attachments, but also to those professionals and parents who are wanting to assist such adolescents. Thank you Floyd, for this exemplary work."

David C. Brown, Ph.D., LMFT
Owner of Deseret Counseling Center

"Finally, a scientifically supported book that addresses sexuality through the lens of attachment wounds and needs. Floyd has studied the research, ignored the politics, and speaks to the deeper issue. This book will have life changing effects for those choosing Recovery."

John McLean, LPC, CSAT, Psychotherapist

"Floyd Godfrey's book Healing and Recovery shines a light on the many confusing and challenging parts of young men's journey of identity and sexual development. Many young men struggle with emotional turmoil and belonging, a flood of sexual feelings and thoughts, and a lack of maturity and mentoring toward manhood. Floyd's book is a competent guide for young men to understand the complexity of sexual attraction, to recover from problematic sexual behavior, and to heal relationship wounds. Floyd shares his personal experiences, clinical insights from many years of specialized therapy with those struggling with sexual issues, and what science reveals about sexuality and attachment. The book reminds the reader to not accept societal labels, but rather honor oneself by slowly and carefully practicing self-discovery. The world needs young men who are confident and see themselves accurately. This book provides a solid path to this end. "

Shane Adamson LCSW, EFT, CSAT
Director, Center For Marriage & Family Counseling
Podcast Host, Help for Loving Relationships

"In my work with individuals across the sexual orientation spectrum, rarely do I find a person who has not experienced an attachment wound. It is often the case that these attachment wounds shift our thinking patterns, alter behavioral patterns, and can lead to painful feelings such as depression and anxiety. When a person begins to understand the nature of their attachment needs, and finds healthy ways to get those needs met that are congruent with their value system, peace can be found and greater joy experienced. Floyd's book explores the concepts of attachment as it relates to sexual fluidity and identifies key elements of attachment that aid in a deeper understanding of one's feelings, desires, and behaviors."

Troy L. Love, LCSW, SATP
Author of "Finding Peace"

"This workbook is in many ways, a whole-hearted approach to understanding the etiology of attachment disruptions and how they can manifest in numerous ways throughout one's life. This work is both empirically supported and consistent with the clinical work that is expected of a contemporary therapist. Floyd's book shines a light on an issue that permeates the fabric of society, and he illuminates the material in a way that illustrates his passion and concern for those who struggle with and toward recovery."

Eric Schultz, MFT, CSAT, Psychotherapist

Acknowledgements

This workbook came about through the multitude of clients who helped me develop an understanding of sexualized attachments. The presenting frustration and confusion magnified my desire to understand this topic more completely.

I'm also grateful to various colleagues who made this project possible and provided invaluable input and feedback. I appreciate your time, effort, and honesty. Your helpful criticism was essential in the research and format of this project: Dr. Maylin Batista, Dr. Mary Anne Fifield, and Dr. Matthew Hedelius. Additionally, I feel very blessed for the tutelage of Dr. Monica Breaux who inspired me to think in new ways and analyze the research from a different perspective. Thank you for your faith, patience and time with me on this project.

A special thank you to my bride, Kaleen, who allowed me to work, write, and complain. She listened to my doubts and hesitations. A huge thank you to my brothers and sister who encouraged and supported various aspects of this work. Finally, a big thank you to my children who were forced to live with a father who was always talking about sexuality research and, sometimes, embarrassing them in public.

Table of Contents

Rationale for this Workbook

I've worked as a professional therapist with hundreds of men, women, and youth who have sexualized attachments. Usually, these clients came to my office expressing pain, conflict, and confusion. They often struggled with childhood difficulties that seemed relevant to their confusion. They shared private and sometimes traumatic stories of events they insisted had contributed to their pain.

My attention was piqued when Dr. Lisa Diamond wrote her book in 2008 about sexual fluidity.[1] In it she discussed her observations that some women shift attraction toward either a man or a woman. This shift for some individuals pointed her toward the concept of sexual fluidity. Dr. Diamond observed that for some women love and desire are not rigidly heterosexual or homosexual. She repeated her position in 2017 and stated: "There are genetic influences, but they are not deterministic. There is a lot evidence for fluidity and change in people's experiences of same-sex attraction."[2]

Her research enhanced my own clinical observation that some people's sexuality was influenced by various emotional dynamics. As I explored this issue, concepts of secure-attachment, insecure-attachment, defensive-detachment, and anxious-attachment kept coming up in the research. As did the concept of sexualized attachments that includes issues such as trauma bonding, trauma repetition, and trauma re-enactment.

I was again intrigued when Ritch Savin-Williams published his book "Mostly Straight" in which he explored sexual fluidity among men. He asserted the same observation as Lisa Diamond and explored biological and psychological factors that combine to influence sexual attraction.[3]

Similarly, Neil King observed emotional patterns which influenced sexuality.[4] He noticed that arousal patterns were often developed through emotional dynamics and, over time, became imprinted.

I spent several years collaborating with other professionals – some who felt

---

1   Diamond, L. M. (2009). *Sexual fluidity: Understanding women's love and desire*. Cambridge, MA: Harvard University Press.

2   Martinez, L. (2017, February 10). Professor strikes down 'born this way' argument for homosexuality. Retrieved from https://badgerherald.com/news/2017/02/10/professor-strikes-down-born-this-way-argument-for-homosexuality/

3   Savin-Williams, R. C. (2017). *Mostly straight: Sexual fluidity among men*. Cambridge, MA: Harvard University Press.

4   King, N. (2000). Childhood Sexual Trauma in Gay Men. *Journal of Gay & Lesbian Social Services,12(1-2), 19-35.* doi:10.1300/j041v12n01_02

strongly about environmental influence, and some who felt strongly about genetic influence. In some instances, these professionals had intensely political or religious beliefs. I listened and learned from both positions and, after more research, decided to write this workbook.

My fear is that adults and youth label themselves as abnormal or broken when they are experiencing symptoms of sexualized attachments. Sometimes people have homosexual, bisexual, or other sexual attractions that we can't assume are inherent. Unfortunately, this seems to be the current assumption of inexperienced clinicians.

In striving for equality, lobbyists and activists have pushed for societal changes to increase acceptance and reduce discrimination. The reduction in discrimination and hatred has made a positive impact on society. However, this cultural climate has created hesitation to examine emotional influence on sexual attraction for fear of professional repercussions. Some clinicians abandon consideration of factors outside genetics for the sake of avoiding political backlash.

In this scenario, clients are labeled based on attraction without a complete understanding of what's happening inside themselves. People who experience sexualized attachments may be completely uneducated about emotional deficits or attachment wounds. They may be living without any awareness of their own unaddressed attachment needs or wounds. This workbook is my effort to help young men and clinicians to understand the symptoms and scope of sexualized attachments and to find healing and recovery.

Foreward

Before You Begin

This workbook is intended to provide you with insight into sexualized attachment issues. You will learn about contributing factors and symptoms of sexualized attachments. I have personally experienced confusion surrounding these difficult issues, and I have worked with hundreds of youth who also struggled. This material is written to help you sort through these challenges.

This workbook can be used as a guide but doesn't replace a real person. It will have minimal impact without support and guidance from others. To make a more lasting impression, I strongly suggest you review this workbook with a professional counselor and with loved ones who can support you. Provide yourself opportunities to connect with others throughout this process and you will find long-term success in your healing. There are various topics covered inside the workbook that may bring up a whirlwind of emotion. Some of the emotions might be new. Having someone with whom you can share will be invaluable as you sort through all the emotions that arise. Some young men feel overwhelmed by the intensity of these issues. This is normal. Don't be afraid to seek out the help you need.

Healing requires connection and bonding with people you love and trust. It requires you to reach out for support. You must experience deeper and more secure attachments that you've been missing. So before you begin… find someone with whom you can share as you read and learn.

Chapter 1

Despair and Hope

I was a young child when I fell into Grandma's swimming pool. I panicked and reached out for something to grab onto, but my body slid beneath the surface of the water. I fought to keep my head up, gasping for air and kicking frantically. Others sat calmly at the edge of the water but didn't see me. I was terrified. I was out of control. I couldn't breathe. Terror swept over my mind.

I felt this same panic when I first noticed sexual curiosity about other boys. I was drowning in a sense of despair that left me confused and depressed. I remember saying to myself: *"Why me? Why would God do this to me?"* I spent years floundering in confusion until a mentor reached out to me. He himself had nearly drowned in similar confusion. He had struggled with sexual addiction and confusion from a young age. But with persistence in recovery, he discovered emotional needs and wounds underneath his addiction. With the help of his wife, a good therapist, and support from his friends, he worked on these root issues and found a pathway to healing and recovery. I was blessed to know him.

My own journey in recovery began at a conference. Men from across the country with various backgrounds and struggles attended the retreat. Most everyone in attendance had struggled with sexual and relational wounds. However, these men didn't seem embarrassed or ashamed. They saw themselves simply as men… this was their only label. They were honest to admit that various wounds and scars fostered diverse sexual temptation. It was evident they had cultivated peace and balance in their lives. They were an inspiration to me.

One of the most inspiring moments at the retreat came with personal testimonies. A man named Jeff stood up and told his own story of promiscuity and isolation. His lifestyle had left him lonely and miserable, leaving him overwhelmed and worn out. As he was crumbling inside, Jeff attempted suicide. But after a couple of failed attempts, he sought help from a professional counselor. He returned to church and found love and support he had not experienced previously. He made a determined effort to find healing and recovery. I was deeply touched by Jeff's story. I could relate to his struggle and his emotion.

Later during the retreat, a therapist explained the concept of sexualized attachments and how to find healing. Hope began to form in my heart. The retreat was life-changing. My entire life I had wrestled with issues I could not grasp. I'd been sidetracked by confusion and shame, and couldn't see the deeper needs and wounds inside my heart. My soul was hungry for connection and friendship; my heart was heavy with a whirlwind of emotion. The discovery of underlying emotional needs became a turning point in my life. Despair turned into hope.

Within this workbook I share my personal experience with recovery from sexual addiction and healing from sexualized attachments. No two stories are identical and mine will not be exactly like your own. You are unique with your own experiences and characteristics. Don't get distracted by any differences in our stories. Look for parallels with your own experiences. I believe as you read and review the questions at the end of each chapter, you will notice ways that our stories are similar. This will give you insight to set goals and find healing.

Remember this is a workbook. Read it thoroughly. There is no need to rush; take your time. Discuss what you are learning with people you trust. Answer the questions at the end of each chapter sincerely and honestly. This will help you see more clearly any issues you need to resolve, or behaviors you need to change. You will become more self-aware as you identify areas of concern.

Good luck on your journey. It's liberating to be free of the confusion, obsessive thoughts, urges, and behaviors. I found healing along with thousands of other men and women. You can too!

Chapter 2

Elementary School

I always felt different but can't pinpoint any specific beginning. My confusion must have started very young. I recall a childhood filled with a whirlwind of emotion. My mother told me I was very sensitive. This made punishment unnecessary because I quickly complied. She knew I was shy and sometimes anxious. With strangers, I clung quietly to her leg and stood behind her. But when surrounded by familiar people I was social and playful.

I remember withdrawing into myself when I started kindergarten. I had barely turned five years old, so I was almost a year younger than most of the other kids. Everything was new and strange and I wasn't sure how to fit in. As I progressed in elementary school, the boys often played rough-and-tumble games during recess. I rarely joined them. I was unfamiliar with their games and afraid of getting hurt.

One day at recess I sat on the ground, pulling at the grass and letting it fall through my fingers as I watched a group of boys play kickball. A couple boys came over and asked if I wanted to play. I felt awkward and didn't know how to answer them. They continued trying to persuade me, so I agreed. We walked over to the other boys and picked teams. Confidence turned to embarrassment when I was the last one chosen. As the game commenced I instinctively felt uncoordinated. I believed everyone was watching and judging me. One boy was tall and very athletic. Everyone seemed to like him. I watched and thought, *"I want to be like him."* I compared myself and was jealous. I felt inadequate and didn't want to play anymore.

I stopped hanging out with boys during recess and found a group of girls. We played jump rope and climbed monkey bars. Sometimes we enacted scenes from *Star Wars*. I always insisted on playing the role of Luke Skywalker because I perceived the character as strong, courageous, and popular. I felt more comfortable with these activities because they were safe and didn't open me up to embarrassment. I could just be myself and didn't have to compete for attention. I established a pattern of avoiding boys and their games, and associating more with girls. It just felt safer.

At the beginning of each new school year the pattern continued. When I was insecure or anxious, I avoided boys and their active games. I established a routine that was comfortable and safe. I chose to play with girls or keep to myself. However, this routine abruptly changed when my family moved to a new city at the end of fifth grade.

My father was very religious and strict about keeping distance from "temptations of the world." He was legalistic in his approach to religion, and our family never missed church services. Moral standards of behavior were very important to him. Likewise, he felt that we should associate only with others of similar values and morals. I interpreted my father's message as an expectation to separate myself from non-Christians; to distance myself from any bad influence.

I watched children in the neighborhood play games together and yearned to be with them. Sometimes they would call out for me to join them, but I always gave some excuse. As I turned my back and walked away, I rehearsed in my mind the true reason I wouldn't play: *"They don't go to church – they don't hold Christian values – I have to be better."* This internal message prevented me from seeing anything in common with kids in the neighborhood or at school. Over time the neighbor kids stopped inviting me to play, and I gradually became isolated.

At the beginning of sixth grade, some of the boys at school started "going-out" with girls. They expressed interest by giving her a nod of the head or passing notes during class. Most of the boys hardly even associated with the girls they were going-out with. Later, I could see that this behavior was simple adolescent exploration, but my parents and church had drilled into me that flirting was hazardous and should wait until high school. I perceived the childish romances as wrong. My moral anxiety was strong. The boys were playing social games. They were curious and innocent – not immoral or sinful. But I wanted to be a "good boy." I sought to do what I believed would please God, and refused to participate in the social games with girls. This moral tension alienated me further from my peers.

This moral anxiety soon created a barrier toward the opposite sex. I only associated with girls on a "friend" level. I was afraid to think of them romantically and was only bonding with them as peers. Conversely, I was anxious and insecure about my connection with other boys, which prevented any deeper emotional association with them. I was definitely more comfortable associating with girls and was anxious about connecting with boys.

Chapter 2 Questions

1. What can you relate to in this chapter? Express yourself with details.

_____

_____

_____

_____

_____

_____

_____

_____

2. My experience with boys at recess had a powerful impact on my life. Have you had similar experiences? Write about any events that stand out in your mind and why they do.

_____

_____

_____

_____

_____

_____

_____

_____

3. What was your experience with the opposite sex in elementary school? How were those feelings different than your feelings and experiences with same-sex peers? Write about one of these memories.

_____

_____

_____

_____

_____

_____

_____

_____

_____

_____

_____

_____

_____

_____

_____

_____

_____

_____

_____

_____

Chapter 3

Junior High School

Opportunities for friendship continued in junior high but I was overwhelmed. Puberty increased my insecurity and anxiety. When I entered seventh grade, I kept to myself and maintained walls with other boys. I hardly recognized anyone when I started junior high. I desperately wanted a best friend and a group of buddies. I wanted to hang out, join in the games, and feel acceptance in the world of boys. I simply wanted to belong.

It was obvious during junior high that some boys were growing faster than others. Some became physically superior and athletically skilled. It never occurred to me that I was almost a year younger than my peers, so I compared myself ruthlessly. I was skinny and small. I was embarrassed about my less-developed body, and kept my shirt on during sports. I didn't want the other boys to tease me about my small chest and arms or lack of body hair.

I remember a boy in PE named Justin who had been lifting weights with one of the coaches at school. Justin was not embarrassed in the locker room. He would strut around without his shirt and flex his biceps to show off. All the boys admired him. He appeared confident and popular. He was an excellent athlete, and everyone wanted to be around him.

Admiration and envy welled up inside me as I realized I couldn't compete with Justin. I wanted to be confident and admired – to be like him. It was a keen emotional attraction to Justin; admiration and envy mixed with a rush of adrenaline.

When I finally started puberty, I became even more self-conscious. I avoided showers at school, but also wanted to be with the guys. The locker room was a place boys would laugh, talk, and joke with one another. It was a social space for them.

One day a boy named Earl invited me to join the wrestling team. I remember listening to his encouragement. I wanted a reason to associate with him and the other young men I envied. I imagined interacting with teammates and having buddies. I imagined being athletic and admired. My heart leaped at the chance to have buddies. I wanted to try but feared the team atmosphere. Despite my fear and insecurity, Earl convinced me to come out for the team.

On the day of the first practice I agonized in worry and fear. I yearned to be with other boys but was scared to death about this new experience. During the first practice I watched the other boys closely. It seemed like everyone knew what they were doing except me. I was the youngest on the team and was obviously smaller and less developed. The team was primarily composed of older boys who were more physically mature.

As the semester progressed, I avoided workouts to hide my clumsiness. Sometimes, the coach gave me extra help. I liked the attention but felt stupid that I was singled out from the others. At wrestling meets I sat quietly on the bench, hoping to be overlooked. I waited anxiously for my turn. I anticipated losing and imagined my own defeat. At one wrestling match, I won by forfeit. It was horrible. I wondered, *"Is forfeit the only way I can win?!"* At this point my self-esteem was sinking, and my mind was filled with shame-talk: *"I'm not good enough; I don't measure up; something's wrong with me; no one likes me the way I am."*

After workouts the whole team was required to shower before going home. The school had a gang shower in the locker room with showerheads on the wall. I was shy about taking my clothes off, so when the team was undressing I would sometimes fake a direction toward the shower, then return to my locker before the coach noticed.

The other boys didn't seem to mind the nudity. They would undress, talk, and joke with each other in the shower. Sometimes they would even tease each other or play games. The coach would eventually come to hand out towels and tell them to hurry. They seemed confident and didn't mind having other boys see them undressed. I wondered how they could be so relaxed. When I did shower, it was evident that other guys had more muscles, body hair, and physical signs of manhood. This only intimidated me and increased my jealousy because I was younger and less developed. It increased my sense of being different from everyone else. I wanted to be a part of the team, but my fears drove me away.

That was my last year of wrestling. At the end of seventh grade, my family moved across the country. I started a new school in another state and things began to improve. I played the piano and became very musical. My circle of friends began to expand and I became more comfortable in groups, though I still found myself sitting on the sidelines more often than I wanted. I frequently watched other boys play sports and could feel the admiration, envy, and comparisons growing inside my heart.

I dreamed about myself as more athletic, more developed, more outgoing, more social, and more muscular – and became increasingly preoccupied with these thoughts. I often sat in class and fantasized about having the perfect body, pitching on a baseball team, singing solos in choir, and having buddies who admired me. I even started to idolize the way boys interacted together. I created in my mind the image of what a "cool" guy should be: outgoing, popular, sports-oriented, good looking, and physically developed – everything I believed that I was NOT. My concept of ideal masculinity did not match my self-perception. My concept of gender seemed incongruent with who I really was.

Chapter 3 Questions

1. What can you relate to in this chapter? Go into detail.

_____

_____

_____

_____

_____

_____

_____

_____

_____

2. How does your perception of an "ideal man" compare to your perception of yourself?

_____

_____

_____

_____

_____

_____

_____

_____

_____

3. Do you ever feel inferior or insignificant to others of the same sex? Please describe.

_____

_____

_____

_____

_____

_____

_____

_____

_____

_____

4. How do your experiences with same-sex peers impact the activities you choose to participate in?

_____

_____

_____

_____

_____

_____

_____

_____

_____

_____

5. Have you ever had experiences in the locker room that caused confusion or discomfort? What happened?

_____

_____

_____

_____

_____

_____

_____

_____

_____

_____

Chapter 4

High School

When I started high school, I feared something was wrong with me. Emerging sexual feelings confused me. The sensation was both exciting and disgusting. My parents never taught me about sex or puberty and the lack of information created obsessive questions and curiosity. I didn't understand the urges and was embarrassed about them. Often my curious thoughts included boys I admired or envied. In my fantasies, I became one of the guys. I longed for male friendship. I hungered for buddies and best friends. This emotional hunger was morphing into something sexual.

When I turned fifteen, I was anxiously determined to visit my Bishop for spiritual advice. I quietly requested a time to visit and went to his office. I rehearsed in my mind what to say. The door opened and I was invited inside. We sat down and he offered some light conversation. Then he asked me, *"What can I do for you?"*

I hung my head and fidgeted uncomfortably in my chair. This would be the first time I had ever told anyone about my confusion. It would be the first time I had ever spoken out loud about the issue. I was terrified and my stomach hurt. I wasn't sure how to describe the sexual feelings, so in a quiet hush I said, *"I might be gay."*

The bishop wasn't startled and responded calmly, *"Why do you think you are gay?"* His gentle response was reassuring, and he seemed to honestly care.

"Well..." I stammered, *"I have sexual thoughts about the other boys. I don't know what to do. Can you help me?"* I told him about the daydreams and attractions. He was patient and listened well. I shook in fear of what he might think of me. I had always portrayed an image of a good Christian kid, but now someone would know the truth. I was mixed-up and confused, perhaps even a disappointment. How would he feel about me after this revelation? I waited for his response and some dire criticism.

To my surprise he responded with love and compassion. He said, *"Most boys your age have sexual feelings that might be confusing. The feelings are new to you. You're not used to them. It's normal. Let's pray together, stay close to the Lord, and trust Him."* I felt some of my burden lifted and a sense of relief that he wasn't judging me.

Unfortunately, his words of comfort were temporary as my loneliness, jealousy, envy, discontent, and hunger to connect with other boys intensified. My emotions were in turmoil. I was confused and alone. My preoccupation increased.

I put on a happy face and continued to develop talents in music. I joined the swim team but avoided most team-sports. Somehow swimming felt safer than sports like basketball or football. I felt better about myself, but part of my life was empty. I yearned to connect with other young men. I was desperately missing male community.

As for my parents, the distance with my father continued to grow, while I maintained an especially close relationship with my mother. Sometimes the distance with my dad turned into anger and resentment. My father never seemed to listen and rarely admitted mistakes. He was closed-minded, rigid, and very opinionated. This became a constant source of irritation to me. My father easily communicated criticism and negativity. Nothing I accomplished ever seemed good enough for him. My father kept busy with work and showed little interest in my personal life.

This dynamic sprouted a terrible character flaw – I started holding grudges. I would ponder for days on the criticism and disdain from my dad. I became obsessed and angry about it. My father's absence in my personal world was profound. I was starved for a mentor in my life, and left to fend for myself. Over time it became easier to distance myself from my father. He made few attempts to reach out unless it was to interview me about obedience to gospel teachings. He wanted to ensure that I didn't fall into sinful behavior, so he would periodically check up on me. My father was constantly absorbed in his career. He often brought work home and seemed endlessly preoccupied or tense – unapproachable.

He was also easily angered. He was the dictator in our family and ran the household with authoritarian style. No one dared question or petition against his wishes. He could not accept criticism, admit to any wrong, or apologize for any reason.

I was afraid of my father and remember an occasion when he had been cleaning the garage. Somehow, he was blaming me for misplacing his hammer. However, within a few minutes he found the hammer he'd been missing. So, as a surly young teen, I commented, *"So it was your fault? How does it feel to be wrong?"* He responded by kicking me across the driveway. His hard-toed shoe was painful, and I cried inwardly because it embarrassed me. But I refused to let my father see any display of pain. I denied him that satisfaction.

I never really knew my father... or let myself know him. I realized later that my father used intimidation to keep all the family members in line. He was quick to shame and induce fear upon us.

In high school, I met with my new Bishop for spiritual help. I couldn't talk to my

HEALING & RECOVERY

father and preferred to talk with someone else. While my father was condescending, my church leaders always expressed encouragement and support. They seemed patient and caring. I believed the teachings of the Bible, so prayed continuously for God's intervention. My faith was strong, and I assumed that God and some miraculous event could help me with my sexuality.

One night after a discouraging day, I knelt by my bed to pray. Confusing sexual thoughts about other young men had become stronger and more obsessive. I was emotionally drowning and felt alone. In prayer I pleaded: *"Please God... tell me what to do! Please God... don't abandon me."*

I couldn't stop the emotion and sobbed by the bedside. *"I don't want to be like this. I want to be like the other boys. I want to get married and have a family. I want you to be pleased with me. I am lost."* Once the tears slowed down, I laid my head on the side of the bed. After several minutes, a quiet peace came over me. I heard very gentle thoughts inside my mind: *"It will all be okay. I am here."* My sniffling subsided as I took the message to heart.

I turned back to prayer to continue the conversation: *"I want to trust you God, but what should I do?"*

No response.

"Please God... what should I do?"

Nothing. Silence. Finally, after some moments of delay, I determined that I would simply remember those words as a way of maintaining hope: *"It will all be okay."* I picked myself up and crawled into bed. I was emotionally drained and exhausted.

As the school year finished, sexual thoughts entered my mind constantly and powerfully. It was obsessive. I redirected the thoughts toward other things and tried to sing hymns, memorize Bible verses, or similar distractions. I dated girls, but never found romance. The idea of kissing a girl was disgusting. Girls seemed like sisters, friends, and mothers, not the object of romance or sexual activity. On the other hand, I hungered for the attention and affection of young men. Wherever I went, I began to fantasize about boys and men.

After my high school graduation, the family moved again. I didn't feel ready to go to college on my own, so I went with them. I tried to fit into a new neighborhood and church. I was invited to serve on a mission trip, but I had labeled myself as bad and unworthy. Several other young men within the church would be going, but I felt spiritually inferior. I told myself that God wouldn't want me to go; that God doesn't want sexually confused people in ministry.

When I turned eighteen, I once again disclosed my secrets to the new bishop at our new church. Like the others, he was loving and compassionate. After learning that I had not disclosed anything to my parents, he urged me to share my struggle with them. He assured me they should know, to provide support. I was horrified by the idea. *"No way! This is awful and they will NOT respond well."* I struggled with the advice for several weeks. I prayed about it. To imagine the potential conversation brought terror and I feared their response.

I considered in my mind other alternatives. I analyzed options and finally narrowed it down to three possibilities:

1) Run away secretly where my family would never find me.

2) Kill myself so my parents would never know about my secrets.

3) Tell them about everything and ask for support.

Running away didn't seem like an option - I had nowhere to go. Killing myself seemed easier, but I was afraid it would be painful, and I might go to hell. Ultimately, I saw no other option but to tell my parents. With the Bishop's reassurance, I decided to tell them.

I focused on my "good qualities" as a way of gaining courage to tell my parents about what I was experiencing. By all outward appearances I had made good decisions – I was a "good kid." I never created problems at school. My grades were excellent, and I had received a full-ride scholarship to a local university. I performed well in school activities, and everyone seemed to like me. Religious leaders thought I was a terrific role-model for the younger kids. I went to church every Sunday and tried to be a good Christian, living biblical standards of behavior. I served in the children's ministry and generally tried to volunteer.

My relationship with my mother had always been close. I trusted her and felt safe with her. I sincerely believed she would understand the dilemma and have compassion. On the other hand, I was apprehensive about creating more sadness for her. I had already witnessed so much sorrow from her relationship with my dad. Because of my father's cold and manipulative manner, she often pulled away from him. I had guessed we were both afraid of him and weary of his insensitive nature. Her compassion in the past gave me courage to speak openly and ask for help. I knew that I was special to her, and confident she would help me work through these challenges.

Finally, I asked my parents for some time. I ushered them into my room.

Nausea filled my stomach as they came in to sit down. My heartbeat sent echoes throughout my body. I was gasping for air. I cleared my throat and sat on the edge of my bed. Awkwardly I stammered, *"I think I'm gay."* I sat in agony looking at them and waiting for a response.

With a quizzical but firm glare, my father replied, *"No you're not!"* My mother hung her head and bit her nails. Her eyes filled up with tears. I went completely numb and unable to speak another word. My parents asked some questions, but the rest was a blur. I was in shock. My father was in complete denial, and my mother was emotionally overwhelmed. This event transpired exactly the way I imagined - father unable to listen or understand, and mother quietly confused. The only silver-lining was the potential for professional counseling. That very night my mother called the church, and I was referred to a therapist at social services.

My father didn't speak about the issue again until a few days later when he took me for a drive. He wanted clarification. We drove down a lonesome road through a canyon outside the city. I sat in silence as the car sped along. I was racked with shame, tension, and feeling vulnerable. Breaking the stillness, my father asked, *"Do you understand what you've said?"* In a tone of disgust, he wanted to know if I understood the implications. He graphically described homosexual behavior and stated, *"...that's disgusting...but that appeals to you?"*

His statements were harsh and cold. His tone frightened me and I sat silently. Memories of life-long intimidation flooded over me – I was panicked. I was hoping to avoid further inquisition. Intrusive thoughts flashed through my mind about getting pushed from the car or abandoned in the desert. He had already abandoned me emotionally, so the intrusive thoughts didn't seem crazy. My stomach was knotted up and sick. I didn't know what to do. He had me trapped inside the car. I tried to fend off the questions by lying. I minimized the confusion, but he wouldn't stop his questions. In a strangled voice, I told him I wanted to go home. Rather than attempt to understand, he lectured me the rest of the drive.

The torment ended when we arrived home. I could see my mother's questioning eyes as I shuffled down the hall to my room. I was too shaken to cry, so I lay on the bed feeling numb and alone. I didn't want to talk to anyone. *"Couldn't my mother have seen this coming? Couldn't she have done something to prevent the confrontation and humiliation?"* I spent the rest of the day in my room. Isolated. Alone. Uncertain. Depressed. Abandoned.

Soon thereafter, my parents sent me to a counselor widely known for his work with teens. He provided insights and uplifted me at every session. It was nice to have someone listen without criticizing or judging. I felt relief in talking and it freed me from some of the shame. Unfortunately, basic talk therapy was insufficient to give me insight into the confusion. The counselor's lack of training on the topic prevented progress. Visits with this counselor did not help to heal emotional wounds or resolve attachment issues. There was no recovery insight. I'm guessing the counselor didn't even know basic recovery concepts.

After about a year of counseling, I just stopped going. It wasn't helping. This same counselor admitted several years later that he didn't know anything about sexual addiction or sexualized attachments and was simply trying to encourage me.

Chapter 4 Questions

1. What can you relate to from this chapter? Write down similar feelings or experiences that you have. Go into detail.

_____

_____

_____

_____

_____

_____

_____

_____

_____

2. Does this chapter bring up issues that are STILL a problem? What issues are bothering you NOW?

_____

_____

_____

_____

_____

_____

_____

_____

3. Do same-sex peers participate in activities that you avoid?

_____

_____

_____

_____

_____

_____

_____

_____

_____

4. Describe the relationship with your own father.

_____

_____

_____

_____

_____

_____

_____

_____

_____

5. Describe the relationship with your own mother.

_____

_____

_____

_____

_____

_____

_____

_____

_____

_____

6. What are the differences in your relationship with each parent?

_____

_____

_____

_____

_____

_____

_____

_____

7. What would it take for you to confide with someone about your confusion?

_____

_____

_____

_____

_____

_____

_____

_____

_____

_____

_____

Chapter 5

Finding Answers

After my first year of college, I left for a mission trip to South America. I was filled with enthusiasm and hope. I wanted to please God. I wanted to teach the gospel and serve people, but I also hoped that God would magically cure my sexual preoccupation. I prayed that He would bless me for devoting this time to serve and share the gospel. I was very transactional, expecting to earn magical blessings. I didn't understand grace and was trying to earn my sense of value.

Before leaving, I was required to meet with a professional therapist to assess my emotional stability. I was hesitant due to my previous experience with counseling. But I complied so that the church could review my application. The counselor found me to be mentally stable and the church allowed me to participate. At this point, I believed that only God himself could heal me of my sexual preoccupation and I hoped this mission trip might be an opportunity to earn God's blessing.

I traveled to South America and lived among the people. I struggled with sexual urges throughout my stay. Sometimes sexual thoughts possessed my mind and I found it difficult to keep a spiritual tone. However, I stayed busy and occupied myself in service. I worked in soup kitchens, built homes, organized church services, and generally taught the people gospel concepts. It was a rewarding and growing experience. I served diligently and prayed fervently that God would be pleased with my offering. Caught up in a gospel of prosperity, I continued to believe that through obedience I would be healed.

Upon my return I realized, sadly, that the sexual impulses had not changed. To my dismay the miraculous transformation had not taken place. I had worked hard for God, and He had not cured me. My faith in God began to flounder. I met with another counselor and encountered the same dead-end. No one seemed to understand me.

At this point I considered that I might be sexually abnormal. I couldn't shake the feeling that something was going on inside my head. I experienced sexual curiosity about other young men, but it simply didn't feel like my identity.

One day after another fruitless counseling session, the new therapist told me about a support group sponsored by men who struggled with sexual addiction. The counselor wondered if perhaps I might find some answers with other men who struggle with sexuality. I decided it couldn't hurt to see what they had to say. I approached the group with skepticism and doubt.

Surprisingly, the group taught me concepts which changed my life. Starved for answers, I finally found nourishment. It was a turning point. It was the first time I'd heard anyone speak of recovery concepts in a way that made sense. It wasn't about magical cure or change – it was about *healing* and *recovery*. It was about learning to do life differently. There was less focus on sexual thoughts, and more focus on healthy living. There was lots of talk about emotional needs and wounds – finding growth and healing. It was about learning to acknowledge unmet needs and growing through pain and trauma.

Hearing stories from men who understood recovery gave me hope. These men found peace in their lives by living recovery concepts. There was no magic, just hard work. I found myself resonating with every word from these mentors. During one point in the group meeting, pain and emotion came spilling out. I found myself shaking and holding back tears, so I stepped out into the hallway to take a break.

Out in the hall I saw one of the men who taught the lesson that day. He had been the first to tell his story about a life of promiscuity and misery turned into a life of joy and peace. He was about ten years older than myself, and I could relate to him the most. He felt like the big brother I'd never had. Our stories and background seemed incredibly similar. I walked over to thank him for sharing. After all, it must have been hard for him to tell his story. As I approached, he turned to face me. I stood there a moment, but no words would come out - I simply began to cry. With great compassion he put his arms around me and said, *"It will be alright. You can do this."* I collapsed into the arms of this healthy mentor. We talked for a few more minutes and he continued to give me hope. Later, I would look back on that experience as the first of many encouraging moments.

Over the next several years I worked earnestly to apply recovery concepts in my life. I experienced deep challenges and struggles. It took me several years of hard work. I was sometimes discouraged by my own bad choices. Sometimes I felt preoccupied by sexual urges and found it difficult to control myself. At these moments life seemed impossible to imagine without sex. I would feel bad and unworthy and couldn't imagine how anyone could love me. But I kept getting up and working on my recovery program. I wanted to live healthy and find peace. I didn't want to give up.

I was refreshed by new mentors along my journey. Once I was involved in recovery circles, I discovered other men with similar experiences. It was not uncommon for men to have same-sex tendencies and still identify as heterosexual. Sometimes those feelings shifted or diminished during recovery work. But I also learned that shifts in attraction should never be the focus of recovery, but rather my focus should always come back to healthy living. I no longer felt isolated or alone.

Eventually I found a counselor who was more experienced and willing to learn recovery concepts. He was willing to read the materials together with me. Working with an open-minded therapist energized me. He wanted to do more than simply encourage me. We read together about sexual addiction and sexualized attachments. He patiently taught me about attachment drives and helped me expand my self-awareness. We discussed trauma repetition, trauma bonding, and other factors that may have influenced my confusion. He guided me in the process without negatively judging any particular issue.

He supported me and helped me to seek answers. I was deeply grateful for his courage to allow me space to explore my identity. It would have been convenient to label me as gay because I did have sexual urges toward other men. But he followed my lead and asked me to be honest with myself.

I recognized that having the right counselor made all the difference in the world. I was finding answers in the process of good therapy. I learned new recovery concepts and worked hard in their application. I read all the literature I could get my hands on, attended available groups, and consistently attended therapy sessions. I was changing from the inside, and I could feel it.

One day I realized the sexual preoccupation was diminishing. Although sometimes compelling, I fought sexual compulsions vigorously. Slips with sexual addictive behavior were not uncommon and always seemed to set me back into old ways of thinking and feeling. But, despite setbacks I dedicated myself to the process. I kept getting back up. With encouragement from my counselor, I recognized that recovery should always be the main objective for my life. He wisely cautioned me NOT to gauge success on

> **I had sexualized my attachment needs and wounds**

the direction of my attractions. Although he could observe changes happening, he wanted me to stay focused on healing and recovery.

One of the most exciting discoveries in my personal recovery: obsessive sexual attraction had developed through a process of sexualizing attachment needs and wounds.

I had needs for friendship and bonding (attachment) with other young men. My wounds were related to low self-esteem and rejection from men and boys. It took me some time to figure out all the pieces, but once I worked on the emotional roots, recovery became an exciting new adventure. Over time it became obvious that sexual preoccupation was only a symptom. It was a by-product of deeper issues. I missed common growing-up experiences, but this revelation gave me a new spark. It gave me a new direction for the course of my life.

My circle of friends grew as my confidence grew. Dating and socializing became fun and exciting, rather than compulsive or filled with anxiety. After several years, marriage seemed more of a possibility. I met a girl from church and our friendship developed; we began dating. I shared stories with her about my childhood and emotional confusion. I shared my fears about sexuality but, rather than pulling away, she responded with grace and compassion. She shared about her own childhood and private struggles growing up. I felt understood by her and drew closer. The emotional intimacy increased and gently blossomed into romance, so I asked her to marry me.

Marriage has been an important part of my life, but not the final step of recovery. Recovery has been an ongoing process without a finish line. The process takes time. It's more of a marathon than a sprint. At times it can be frustrating and discouraging. Sometimes the sexual confusion has resurfaced, but never with the same obsessive nature. At times I became discouraged, but with compassionate mentors I simply kept working on recovery. There were ups and downs, and I'm grateful for a patient wife who stood by me during struggles. I realize that my sexual addiction has often been overwhelming for her, but she never left and has kept pushing forward.

I feel grateful for the men who encouraged me. Men who paved the road by working their own program of recovery. They could 'walk the talk' because these men had implemented changes in their own lives. I continue to meet other inspiring men from every religion and race.

My wife and I have a wonderful family of three children who bring joy and adventure to our lives. I love my role as father and doing things with my kids: swim meets, flag football, dance competitions, traveling, vacation, camping, swimming, football games, booster clubs, and youth ministry. I love spending time with my bride and feeling her gentle touch as she radiates compassion and patience.

In my previous life, much of my time was caught up in obsession, fantasy, shame, and isolation. Now I relate to men and women in healthy ways. I no longer feel hijacked or manipulated by my own impulses. Recovery provided me mental space to think about God, my wife, my children, my goals, and dreams. This change opened a whole new world for me. It has become a world where I am no longer afraid nor ashamed of who I am. Although sometimes memories of the past resurface, my life reflects values and morals most important to me.

There hasn't been a magical cure or change as I'd originally prayed for, but I thank God for saving me. As a teenager, God told me, *"It will all be okay. I am here."* Now I can see that God has indeed been present the whole time. The journey has been painful, but God has always been there. I'm confident that anyone with a desire for recovery, who puts in the effort, can also receive this joy. It may take longer than you want but, with patience, it is possible.

Chapter 5 Questions

1. What feelings come up for you with this chapter?

_____

_____

_____

_____

_____

_____

_____

2. What questions arise for you about the content of this chapter?

_____

_____

_____

_____

_____

_____

_____

3. Have you ever felt desperate for answers?

_____

_____

4. How do you feel when you hear about the possibility of sexual preoccupation diminishing?

_____

_____

_____

_____

_____

_____

_____

_____

_____

5. What 'unmet emotional needs' might be part of your story?

_____

_____

_____

_____

_____

_____

_____

_____

_____

_____

6. What feelings do you have about God? Do you feel connected to Him? Do you trust Him? Why or why not?

_____

_____

_____

_____

_____

_____

_____

_____

_____

_____

_____

_____

_____

_____

_____

_____

_____

_____

Chapter 6

Defining Sexualized Attachments

There are some important concepts you'll need to understand as you read the rest of this workbook. I'll try to keep it simple but please don't skip the next two chapters. This important information provides some groundwork into the issues that apply to your own situation.

Attachment Needs

Every child is born with innate attachment needs. Essentially this means that everyone instinctively needs connection with other humans. Attachment and bonding are part of our human existence. We are biologically wired for attachment. The attention and nurture provided to infants and children is essential for healthy development and to meet their attachment needs.

Attachment Drives

Attachment drives are the longings we experience toward bonding. This means every child yearns for connection with adult caregivers and peers. It's a survival mechanism. As such, the longing for attachment will persist throughout the lifespan. We have a genetic hunger for deep connection and a sense of belonging.

Attachment Deficits

When ignored or neglected, the need for bonding and connection does not disappear. When attachment needs are left unmet or unfulfilled, it creates emotional challenges. The deficit leaves an emotional void within the child. The unmet needs will persist until they are reconciled.[5] You notice the strength of the attachment drive when mothers take their young children to daycare. Kids often cry due to separation anxiety. They've bonded with mom, not the childcare provider. It requires time and attention from the provider to generate a sense of bonding that ultimately reduces anxiety.

Sometimes children cannot attach due to medical or emotional issues. For example, kids with severe anxiety will have a more difficult time with attachment. Similarly, kids with Autism or RAD (Reactive Attachment Disorder) will have difficulty with attachment.[6] Regardless of obstacles impeding the attachment process, the longing for connection will continue.

It's also important to consider that children have moments throughout the lifespan requiring safe attachment beyond their parents. Boys have general attachment needs to belong with friend-groups. They look for bonding opportunities with same-sex peers; to fit into a group of buddies. Boys desire attachment with mentors: coaches, teachers, etc. Attachment has a larger implication than simply bonding with mom and dad, and includes a sense of belonging.

Attachment Wounds

As children and youth strive toward attachment bonds, they will sometimes experience wounding. Legitimate needs for connection are wounded with experiences such as abuse – physical, emotional, or sexual. Similarly, emotional neglect can have a devastating impact. Wounds and deficits involving attachment leave a child vulnerable to emotional struggles and confusion. One author wrote that beyond actual abuse

---

5   Mooney, C. G. (2010). *Theories of attachment: An introduction to Bowlby, Ainsworth, Gerber, Brazelton, Kennell, and Klaus.* St. Paul, MN: Redleaf Press, p. 22.

6   Karges, C. (2016, August 23). Attachment Issues & Sexuality. Retrieved July 27, 2018, from https://www.addictionhope.com/blog/attachment-issues-sexuality/

or cruelty, parenting styles that disrupt the attachment process contribute to mental health issues later in life.[7]

Sexualized Attachments

Attachment needs and wounds can become "sexualized" when sex is introduced into the equation. For example, if a young boy longs for friendship his attachment needs will be stronger. His legitimate need for connection makes him vulnerable. Perhaps a teenage boy senses this vulnerability and molests him. The abuse hijacks legitimate needs and interjects sexuality. The boy's deep desire for friendship and attention has now been connected to sexuality.

Trauma Reenactment is a more serious form of sexualized attachment. This is when a boy repeats the trauma of what happened to him. For example, the young boy who was abused finds himself as an adult sexually fantasizing in ways that seem to repeat the abuse. His behavior and attractions seem to run parallel to what happened as a child.

Trauma Bonding is a similar form of sexualized attachment. This is when a boy becomes bonded to the event, or to the person initiating the trauma. For example, the young boy who was abused finds himself as an adult sexually behaving or fantasizing in ways with men or women who are like the person who abused him.

Eroticized (Sexualized) Emotions

Some individuals find they have eroticized emotional experiences. Emotions can become sexualized as the energy festers. Strong emotion doesn't have to be traumatic. Strong emotion and attachment-drives are like magnets attracting themselves to sexual energy.

Eroticized Rage has been a way to describe how anger becomes sexualized. Like when someone is acting out in angry ways, perhaps fantasizing about rape or manipulation. Sometimes strippers or exhibitionists report that they sexualized an ongoing need to be "seen" by significant people in their lives. A peeping Tom (voyeur) might report how he sexualized an ongoing need to see into other's lives – that others would let him into their private world. Someone who cross-dresses might report how he sexualized an ongoing need for feminine nurture and affection.

Usually, these emotional dynamics start in childhood. The emotional

---

7   Mooney, C. G. (2010). *Theories of attachment: An introduction to Bowlby, Ainsworth, Gerber, Brazelton, Kennell, and Klaus.* St. Paul, MN: Redleaf Press, p. 20.

climate is strong, feelings are compounded with attachment needs, and the whole pattern becomes sexualized. Not everyone will sexualize these dynamics, but people struggling with sexual confusion often find that it resonates: the rapist sexualized his emotional need for control, the stripper sexualized her emotional need to be seen, the Peeping Tom sexualized his emotional need to see, and the cross-dresser sexualized his emotional need for feminine affection.

Sexualized Attachments – Enlarged Definition

For this workbook, I have enlarged the definition of sexualized attachments to include various forms of eroticized emotion. After working with hundreds of clients on these issues, I cannot ignore the observation that people experience both. Sometimes traumatic scenarios disrupted healthy attachment, and other times emotional experiences were the culprit. Often, they are both happening simultaneously.

In summary, both emotional and attachment dynamics can become sexualized. The stronger the dynamic, and the longer it festers, the stronger its attraction will be toward sexual impulse. Like a magnet, the sexual impulse gets attracted to the emotional or attachment impulse. And once connected, it's difficult to separate.

Does everyone with emotional or attachment wounds sexualize those dynamics? Certainly not. Kids have emotional struggles and attachment wounds but still grow up without sexualized attachment issues or confusion. But those who have experienced sexualized attachments will easily recognize these dynamics.

Chapter 7

Arousal Patterns & Templates

As children, we develop behavior patterns to cope with difficulty and stress. We respond to our circumstances without much control over most situations. We do the best we can to manage. As an illustration, imagine a young boy who lacks attention from his family, and becomes the "class-clown" at school. He learns to gain attention by joking and making classmates laugh. Even when he gets into trouble, the class-clown role helps him to cope with lack of attention at home. He might not realize why he takes on this role. It's simply an attempt to satisfy his hunger for attention and becomes a pattern.

Some patterns grow strong due to various factors. Suppose the boy who lacks attention at home is also uncoordinated. During recess, he's always the last one picked for games. His lack of athleticism doesn't cause him to become the class-clown, but it increases his drive for attention. He now lacks attention both at home and on the playground, so the class-clown pattern grows stronger. He is starved for legitimate attention and his response helps him to satisfy some of the hunger.

Other factors reinforce the cycle. Perhaps he is bullied by older boys, left out of group games, overlooked at church, or some other situation that fuels his hunger for attention. Coping patterns grow stronger when such factors move into the equation. Also, the cycle becomes automatic over time, sort of like a habit. In other words, whenever his hunger for attention grows, the brain moves into the pattern without effort, and he becomes the class clown.

This boy is now spinning in a whirlwind of various thoughts, emotions, and behaviors, and it's the energy of this emotional whirlwind that becomes intertwined with sexual impulses. Like magnetism, sexual energy is drawn into the emotional preoccupation. When emotional and sexual energy are joined, the cycle becomes an "arousal" pattern. Everything moves beyond a simple need for attention, and what was simply emotional now becomes intertwined with sexual.

Returning to our illustration, when the boy is hungry for attention at home and on the playground, he develops the clown-response as a way of satisfying his need for attention. He is increasingly starved for attention. Now suppose this same boy receives an invitation to hang out with an older, teenage boy. He has admired this teen from a distance, and his hunger for connection drives him to accept the invitation.

He finds himself feasting on the attention of this older teenager. The teen wants to spend time with him and helps him to feel important and valuable. He feels new connections in ways he hasn't experienced. The teenager is meeting his need for friendship, attachment, and connection.

One day while hanging out, the teenager pulls up some online pornography and convinces him that its cool. The younger boy is a bit disgusted but intrigued. He hesitates but doesn't want the teenager to be upset, so he concedes. The experience morphs into a game of you-show-me, and over the next few weeks the teen starts initiating sexual games with him. At first the boy was hesitant but certainly didn't want to lose the relationship. He admitted some curiosity and agreed to the games to avoid rejection.

In this illustration, new emotions and urges enter the pattern. The boy's legitimate need for attachment gets hijacked. His deep hunger for time and attention becomes sexualized. His innate need for mentoring and friendship has been confused, and new sexual feelings are introduced.

Now his brain links the need for attention with sexuality. Consequently, whenever his need for attention rises, his sexual feelings also rise. The sexual games with the older teen strengthened the link between emotional and sexual; the games strengthened the arousal pattern. The emotional pattern has been drawn to sexual urges. When he aches for attention he may start to fantasize about sexual games with boys. This ache for attention is a legitimate need for connection that persists throughout the lifespan, but has now been sexualized.[8]

When an arousal pattern is repeated over time, it becomes imprinted. Basically, this means the arousal pattern is getting memorized by the brain on a deeper level. It gets imprinted deeply into the brain as neural pathways are developed. Once imprinted, the brain is now wired for the pattern and it becomes automatic.

Once the pattern has been imprinted, it is called an arousal "template." An arousal template is like a document template. You can write a paper for school using various templates. There are templates for resumes, research papers, agendas, and others. But typically, when you start a new document, your computer will default to the originally established template. Similarly, your brain will revert to the originally established arousal template. We believe the arousal template forms between the ages

---

8   Flores, P. J. (2012). *Addiction as an attachment disorder.* Lanham: Jason Aronson, p.134.

of five and eight, although problems occur when this template becomes distorted.[9] For example, abuse can have a profound impact on the developing template, with a devastating result causing arousal in ways that are not healthy.[10] Any number of templates might be developed and, unfortunately, once it's established it can be difficult to change. Addicts will sometimes talk about images that pop into their mind – as if the images have been seared into their brain.[11] They're not literally burned in, but they have certainly been deeply memorized.

Some researchers will call this "cutting grooves." When patterns are imprinted into the brain, neural pathways are created. These neural pathways are the grooves in the brain. Cutting new grooves will require the repetition of new behavior patterns over time.[12]

This workbook is intended for young men who are confused by sexualized attachments and emotions. When legitimate attachment needs become sexualized, it can create shame or confusion. My clients often described fantasies that did not represent their identity. Similarly, some clients tell me that they are convinced that early experiences shaped their current dilemma.

In some cases, youth question whether they are gay, bisexual, or queer. In an effort to show love and support, people might encourage "coming out." However, just because young people experience sexual attractions to the same sex, does not mean that it's inherent. These attractions can be a byproduct of sexualized attachments, trauma repetition, trauma bonding, or other eroticized emotional dynamics.

This workbook will describe various contributing factors. It was written for adolescents and young men who may have sexualized attachment challenges. It can also be used to help parents, friends, teachers, clergy or counselors learn correct information about how to support those who fit into this category.

This workbook is about healing and recovery. When the arousal template has been influenced by emotional factors, then addressing underlying emotional factors will be essential for healing and recovery. My observation has been that these factors include intrinsic attachment needs and wounds, and forms of eroticized emotion. This observation has been documented by numerous clinicians and social scientists. Neal

---

9   Carnes, P., & Carnes, P. (2001). *Out of the shadows: Understanding sexual addiction.* Center City, MN: Hazelden Information & Edu, p. 88.

10 Carnes, P., & Carnes, P. (2001), p. 88.

11 Carnes, P., & Carnes, P. (2001), p. 91.

12 Katehakis, A. (2010). *Erotic intelligence: Igniting hot, healthy sex while in recovery from sex addiction.* Deerfield Beach, FL: Health Communications, p. 20.

King was one of the first to call the phenomenon an "Imprinted Arousal Pattern."[13]

In the process of healing and recovery, some people report changes in arousal. We do not know to what extent people can experience change but, whether the template changes or not, the focus should always be on healing and recovery. This means satiating needs for attachment which have been unaddressed. It means healing emotional wounds left festering. Success in recovery should not be gauged on whether the arousal template has changed. Anyone struggling with sexualized attachments should strive to become a whole person.

I attended a fascinating presentation about drug use and sexual arousal. The presenter indicated that drugs could hijack the arousal template and morph the template into other avenues. He said the new arousal patterns still exist when clients get off the drugs, but that people must also focus on patterns they want to reinforce.[14] In other words, the template is influenced. We see this clinically, but obviously this should not be the direct focus of treatment planning.

I have worked with hundreds of sex addicts who describe these types of emotional dynamics. They report emotional issues as part of the underlying roots of the addiction. Not everyone with sexualized attachments will be a sex addict, but some report an obsessive quality very much like sexual addiction. It can feel as though you're in a pre-addictive state. In other words, you feel more obsessive because the emotional dynamics inside you are primed for sexual addiction. Any form of acting out could spin into compulsive patterns of sexual activity. Sexualized attachments can be part of the emotional dynamics in which sexual addiction plants itself.

Some young people with sexualized attachments decide to embrace an LGBTQ identity. Others move away from this label for various reasons. Regardless, your emotional healing is important for recovery. You must learn to separate emotions, wounds, and attachment needs from sexuality; to distinguish between the two and find healing. Different emotional influences can pull the stream of sexuality in various directions, but your sexuality should not define you. Be cautious about labels you give yourself.

There are personal questions throughout this workbook that youth can use to learn more about themselves. Anyone reading this workbook should pause and take the time to answer the questions. Think about them. If you are working with a

---

13 King, N. (2000). *Childhood Sexual Trauma in Gay Men. Journal of Gay & Lesbian Social Services*,12(1-2), 19-35. doi:10.1300/j041v12n01_02.

14 Fawcett, D. (2018, May). *Chemsex, Sex Addiction and Men Who have Sex with Men: Effective Strategies.* Speaker presentation of the IITAP Symposium, Scottsdale, AZ.

mentor or counselor, take time to patiently work through personal issues. Discuss them together and find healing solutions. It's time-consuming, so be patient.

Don't get distracted when something does not apply to you. Watch for the issues that apply to your situation and find a trusted adult to talk with about what you're learning. It could be anyone – a parent, family member, coach, mentor, teacher, or religious leader; anyone you trust. Honestly answer the questions and discuss them with this trusted adult. By working through the questions in this workbook you can set goals that provide healing for attachment needs and wounds.

Chapter 7 Questions

1. Children develop behavior patterns as a way of _____ with challenges and stressors.

2. When emotional patterns grow stronger, they can get _____ over time. This means they are embedded more deeply into the brain.

3. Describe how emotional energy and sexual feelings have a type of magnetism about them:

_____

_____

_____

_____

_____

_____

_____

_____

_____

4. What type of emotional energy can attract sexuality?

_____

_____

_____

_____

_____

_____

_____

5. The arousal template is essentially an imprinted _____ pattern the brain has memorized.

6. Your brain will default back to the original template, somewhat like a _____ document.

7. Some boys assume they are gay or bisexual because they have attractions to other boys, when in reality they have _____ attachment issues.

8. Some young men report that their sexual feelings are obsessive, which might be because they are in a _____ emotional state.

9. It's important to remember that sexual urges should not _____ you.

10. What are some important points from this chapter for you?

_____

_____

_____

_____

_____

_____

_____

_____

_____

_____

_____

_____

_____

_____

Chapter 8

Attachment with Parents

Father's Influence

At an early age, children inherently bond with loving parents and caregivers. As they grow, they learn to identify and connect with the same-sex parent — a natural and important stage of development. Boys learn about manhood through fathers and mentors. A father is a boy's model of healthy strength in the world. He has a responsibility to teach his son about healthy masculinity. Good male mentors teach boys about manhood, guiding them into a larger community of men and masculine confidence. This process of connecting with fathers and mentors occurs throughout childhood. Normal attachment-drives pull young boys toward adult men. This attachment need is wired into every child and cannot be ignored, so if this process is disrupted a boy can experience something nicknamed "father-hunger." Secure attachment is essential for healthy development. The rise of "fatherless" homes has created problems for children and changed our society.[15] Research is so obvious on this point that Dr. William Pollack even suggested that schools should assign every boy an adult mentor who can be understanding of his unique interests.[16]

Some boys describe hurtful and abusive relationships with men. In these toxic situations, a boy pulls away from men to keep himself safe. Physical or emotional abuse can have a devastating impact on attachment. Healthy bonding may not occur and emotional hunger for attachment intensifies. The young boy is aching to be close to an adult mentor but cannot get close without feeling unsafe.

---

15 Hunt, J. (Director). (2017). *Absent - One Man Makes a World of Difference* [Video file]. USA: Time & Tide Productions. Retrieved from www.absentmovie.com. A film addressing the wounds left by an absent father.

16 Pollack, W. S. (1999). *Real boys: Rescuing our sons from the myths of boyhood.* New York: Henry Holt and Company, p. 9.

Wounds generated by toxic men often take years to heal. Sometimes the wounds can be directly correlated to self-esteem problems, confidence development, identity problems, and sexual confusion. Dr. James Dobson noted that boys are often in trouble today because their fathers are distracted, workaholics, emotionally exhausted, disinterested, divorced, or unable to cope with life.[17] Fathers may need to seek forgiveness and make changes. Restoring a healthy relationship with his son may take time, patience, and even professional counseling, but should be every father's goal.

Furthermore, boys should never blame themselves for the poor behavior of adults in their lives. I've listened to boys say things like, *"If I had been a better son..."* or *"If I had been more obedient..."* or *"I'm just not lovable the way I am..."* There is NEVER a good reason for a father or mentor to intimidate, manipulate, or abuse in any way. Some people would label this behavior as toxic masculinity and it's not okay. Do NOT fall prey to excuses. If your father refuses to acknowledge responsibility, or make changes in his life, you must move on. With persistence, you can find new mentors who can love and support you. If this is the case with you, search for male mentors who are confident, self-assured, and decisive, as well as kind and compassionate toward you.[18]

On another note, some boys will develop father-hunger due to abandonment. In this scenario, a boy is emotionally hungry for attachment because healthy mentors were never available. Single moms often wrestle with this scenario. Fathers who abandon their families create a nightmare for everyone left behind. Sadly, some fathers pass away prematurely. The unpredictable nature of life often leaves children grieving and starved for guidance. A man's work or military service may require him to leave home. But regardless of good reason, when a boy is left behind, his need for bonding with mentors will go unmet. The innate attachment drive is unsatisfied, and the subtle ache persists inside him. The sexualization of this attachment drive is sometimes obvious.

An author named Shannon Ethridge observed one of her clients who experimented sexually with other men before marrying a woman. He told her that his journey included an emotionally withdrawn father who was absent most of the time.[19] Similarly, I remember one of my teenage clients several years ago who regularly

17 Dobson, J. C. (2005). *Bringing up boys:* Carol Stream, IL: Tyndale House, p. 55.

18 Dobson, J. C. (2005). *Bringing up boys:* Carol Stream, IL: Tyndale House, p. 121.

19 Ethridge, S. (2012). *The Fantasy fallacy: Exposing the deeper meaning behind sexual thoughts.* Waterville, Me.: Christian Large Print Originals, p. 144.

fantasized using pictures of his own father and older men.

Personality differences can be another common obstacle for secure attachment with a father-figure. Sometimes father and son have a disposition completely opposite one another, or diverse interests and hobbies. These opposing features can inhibit emotional connection between parent and child, making it harder for them to relate to one another. When this happens, the need for bonding is unsatisfied and the subtle ache for attachment persists.

Defensive-Detachment

Sometimes a child pulls away to keep himself safe from highly emotional or toxic situations. This process is called defensive-detachment. It's a step further away from simply disconnecting. Rather than forming an attachment bond, the child protects himself by putting up walls against attachment. Detachment can happen with any significant male relationship: uncles, brothers, grandfathers, scoutmasters, neighbors, family friends, coaches, clergy, or teachers. When a boy defensively-detaches from mentors, his need for connection will be unsatisfied. Boys need men, so this emotional need for a boy to attach with male mentors can later become sexualized.

It would be logical to say that defensive-detachment is a way the boy protects himself from what he perceives to be hurtful. It is a natural response to defend himself from the pain of rejection, or the hurt caused by abuse or lack of nurture.

One of my friends in recovery made an interesting observation: *"Sometimes fathers offer love, but their son blocks it from being received."* A boy needs a role model - someone to admire and pattern his life after. He needs someone to imitate and affirm his own masculinity. He needs attachment and identification with a father-figure. For some boys, one unintentional mistake by their father could create a defensive-detachment that cripples their connection. The boy reacts defensively and blocks the father's attempts at future connection.

The defensive-detachment starts with a basic father-son relationship. A boy's *perception* of hurtful events is the key. Sometimes detachment can be buried so deep that he is barely aware it exists. In the end, a boy desperately desires the approval, acceptance, validation, and love of a mentor, but blocks himself from it to keep safe.

Mother's Influence

For most children it's a simple process to bond with their mother as she coddles, breastfeeds, and physically nurtures her child from infancy. A boy's attachment with his mother is essential for healthy development. But as he grows, he will recognize similarity with his father and begin an identification process, which usually includes an increased desire to connect and bond with him.

Despite a desire to protect her son, a growing boy transitions from the safety of his mother to healthy attachment with his father, male mentors, and other boys. Sometimes a loving mother with good intentions might become overly involved with her son. She might become unnecessarily protective. An overly-attached, anxious mother doesn't allow him to leave her side and can inhibit him from bonding with his father. It could also discourage him from bonding with other men or boys. In some instances, a mother may have negative feelings about the boy's father. I've heard young men describe how their mom was extremely critical or demeaning about their father. Phrases like, *"Don't ever be like your dad,"* or *"Men are so hurtful and uncaring... you better not grow up to be like that!"*

Whether she says it out loud or simply thinks about it, a child will sense the negativity. Children perceive the energy. They can feel the criticism and contempt for men and their fathers. A boy doesn't want to hurt his mother and may subconsciously try to avoid doing whatever his father did. Furthermore, he might unconsciously avoid becoming like his father (whatever that might be) to prevent further pain for his mother. Dr. James Dobson noted that a mother holds the key to the relationship between father and son. "If you show respect to him as a man, they will be more likely to admire and emulate him."[20] A mother's influence can hinder or encourage a boy's connection with his dad and healthy male mentors.

---

20 Dobson, J. C. (2005). *Bringing up boys.* Carol Stream, IL: Tyndale House, p. 94.

HEALING & RECOVERY

Detachment & Sexual Abuse

The topic of sexual abuse is discussed later in this book. However, I want to briefly mention that sexual abuse or molestation can activate defensive-detachment. Abuse adds another layer of pain and confusion. Boys are naturally hungry for approval, affirmation, and affection. When these legitimate needs are hijacked, it may create wounds and emotional confusion about those natural needs.

Sexually abused kids may already have an insecure-attachment toward one or both parents and are more susceptible to abuse by a perpetrator. Sexual predators watch for easy prey. They can sense it within the victim.

If you've been sexually abused or molested, then your natural needs for approval, affirmation, and affection were hijacked. It's painful, confusing, and unfair, but don't despair. Make sure you work through the information in the chapter about sexual abuse.

The Perception Filter

Perception is how we filter life experiences; how we see and perceive the world around us. It's possible that a boy could disconnect or detach from people simply due to his own mental filter. There are a multitude of reasons a boy might perceive emotional hurt or neglect. A father could have the best intentions, but if a child interprets his behavior as negative, then the child will pull away. The following is a list of possible perceptions and responses that could lead to attachment deficits:

- Father is perceived as mostly absent… so the boy lacks attachment because he feels alone.

- Father is perceived as inefficient… so the boy disconnects because he feels frustrated.

- Father is perceived as hostile… so the boy detaches in fear or anxiety.

- Father is perceived as abrasive… so the boy detaches because he feels criticized.

- Father is perceived as abusive… so the boy detaches because he feels violated.

- Father is perceived as uninterested… so the boy detaches because he feels un-loved.

In summary, the boy pulls away and detaches to protect himself. His attachment needs for a mentor are left unsatisfied. The longing in his heart remains.

Broken Filters

A person's perception of reality *is* reality for that person. Although in my life there were moments of obvious manipulation, criticism, and emotional neglect by my father, other situations were likely not intended to be hurtful. But because my father had already hurt me emotionally, I filtered every ongoing interaction as hurtful and I chose to pull away from him.

My father worked excessively and wasn't home much. A strict disciplinarian, he made it clear that we were not to challenge his authority. We weren't allowed to have our own opinions—unless he agreed with those opinions. As a child, I followed his counsel obediently and did not question him. He didn't hesitate to spank and I recall being slapped on some occasions. I was physically afraid of my father and that fear prevented me from connecting with him.

My fear and insecurity about him grew into a general apprehension about men. My filter was broken and I started to see most men as hurtful. My filter generalized the perception of my father toward all men.

When entering fifth grade, I didn't want to be transferred to the new teacher because he was a man. I liked female teachers best because I was more comfortable with women. They were gentle and sensitive to my feelings. I was developing an anxious-avoidant attachment pattern with men that would carry on into college.

Years later, as an adult, I confronted my father about the childhood anxieties and his harsh interaction with me. I'll never forget his bewilderment. He remarked, *"I would never have hurt you."* But it was impossible for me to believe.

To illustrate the concept of broken filters, imagine a young man in a car with his father driving down a long winding road. He wants more than anything to be accepted by his father yet feels nervous. As his father drives, the young man begins to think about their relationship. Staring out the window he notices the beautiful landscape. He sees rolling hills covered with bright, green grass bordering a small stream that stretches over the horizon. Bright, beautiful flowers sway gently in the breeze. The boy says, *"Wow! Dad, did you see that? There was a herd of deer on the grass by that creek!"* Amazed by the scenery he adds, *"This place is awesome!"*

His father, sitting in silence the whole time, turns his head to look out his own window and immediately responds, *"This place is trash."*

Now before finishing the story consider some questions. If this happened to you, how would you feel? Is there anything about this story that reminds you of your own life? Has anything in this story stirred emotion that you've felt before?

The experience of this boy mirrors the experience of young men who experience father-hunger. Experiences like these push a wedge between father and son. For some young men, these experiences are upsetting or traumatic. Before you continue reading, take some time right now to write about your reaction to this story.

Journal Writing

My reactions to the story of the boy in the car.

_____

_____

_____

_____

_____

_____

_____

Now let's continue our story:

Years later when the young man grew up and left home, he remembered this experience in the car and how he allowed it to poison his relationship with his father. He never talked to his father about it. Nor did he try to get an explanation.

When his father died, and the young man (now a grown adult) drove home from the funeral, he found himself on the same road he remembered as a child. He flashed back to the memory and saw the same rolling hills and beautiful grass. He sighed deeply, remembering his father's abrasive comment. As he drove along, he noticed the driver's side of the road and looked out to see his father's view. This side of the road was barren and dry without water. The view was gray and brown. An old, dilapidated factory appeared marked by graffiti and profanity. His father's side of the road looked nothing like the side of the road the young boy observed years previous. The boy and his father never saw what the other had seen. Each was observing a completely different panorama.

From this story, we learn three important lessons. First, a father has a responsibility to connect with his son and guide him to healthy manhood. If he doesn't take the time to listen and seek to understand his son's experiences, a wound in their relationship may be produced that is difficult to heal. The ability to understand his son and relate to him should be a top priority for every father. Whether intentional or not, the gap in their relationship will exist. It will take courage for a father to humble himself, ask forgiveness, and seek to understand.

Second, we learn that a young boy deeply desires his father's approval. Every boy wants to be important and significant to his father. When this approval is not found, it leaves him insecure. Sadly, the young boy in the story allowed the wound to fester and worsen over time. His lack of connection with his father became more pronounced.

Third, the young boy must acknowledge his own broken filter. His father may not have intended to hurt him, but merely saw a different panorama. The father may never have known his words had injured his son. The boy judged his father to be insensitive and harsh. In choosing to remain silent, the boy never gave his father a chance to explain, respond or attempt to heal the injury. He was too young to understand, but the boy's broken filter strengthened the attachment barriers.

In summary, there may be numerous reasons a young man lacks sufficient attachment with fathers and mentors. It could involve physical abuse, emotional abuse, abandonment, mother issues, critical women, death of a loved one, perception of hurt, or other factors that pull the boy away from connection and secure attachment. Regardless, when a boy is left emotionally disconnected, he will be forced to pursue other mentors, or flounder aimlessly on his own.

Chapter 8 Questions

1. Mark any perceptions you have of your father:

❑ Harsh   ❑ Absent   ❑ Abusive   ❑ Uncaring

❑ Rough   ❑ Busy   ❑ Abrupt   ❑ Insensitive

❑ Avoidant   ❑ Weak   ❑ Cruel   ❑ Domineering

❑ Angry   ❑ Critical   ❑ Negative   ❑ Uninvolved

2. How do these perceptions make it hard to connect with your dad?

_____

_____

_____

_____

_____

_____

_____

_____

3. Mark any perceptions you have of *other* adult men:

❑ Harsh   ❑ Absent   ❑ Abusive   ❑ Uncaring

❑ Rough   ❑ Busy   ❑ Abrupt   ❑ Insensitive

❑ Avoidant   ❑ Weak   ❑ Cruel   ❑ Domineering

❑ Angry   ❑ Critical   ❑ Negative   ❑ Uninvolved

4. Who are the men that you perceive this way?

❑ Teachers   ❑ Athletes   ❑ Grandparents   ❑ Actors

❑ Clergy   ❑ Coaches   ❑ Club Leaders   ❑ Family Friends

❑ Brothers   ❑ Neighbors   ❑ Instructors   ❑ Scout Leaders

❑ Uncles   ❑ Teachers   ❑ Youth leaders   ❑ Family Members

5. How do these perceptions make it hard to connect with adult men?

_____

_____

_____

_____

_____

_____

_____

6. Write about a time when it was hard to connect with your father.

_____

_____

_____

_____

_____

_____

_____

7. Write about a time when it was hard to connect with other adult men.

_____

_____

_____

_____

_____

_____

_____

_____

8. Mark any perceptions you have of your mother:

❑ Harsh   ❑ Absent   ❑ Abusive   ❑ Uncaring

❑ Busy   ❑ Insensitive   ❑ Abrupt   ❑ Uninvolved

❑ Avoidant   ❑ Weak   ❑ Cruel   ❑ Domineering

❑ Angry   ❑ Critical   ❑ Negative   ❑ Man-hating

❑ Soft   ❑ Safe   ❑ Rough   ❑ Overly involved

❑ Nurturing   ❑ Dramatic   ❑ Emotional   ❑ Smothering

9. How do these perceptions make it hard to connect with your mother?

_____

_____

_____

_____

_____

_____

10. How do these perceptions make it hard to create a healthy boundary with your mother?

_____

_____

_____

_____

_____

_____

_____

_____

11. How have your experiences changed your perceptions of girls?

_____

_____

_____

_____

_____

_____

_____

_____

_____

_____

_____

_____

_____

_____

Chapter 9

Attachment with Same-Sex Peers

The need for attachment is critical. No human being can escape the biological drive for bonding. We are intrinsically motivated to seek connection. Researcher Philip Flores said that human beings are hard-wired to need people.[21] He believes this need has biological roots inside our brain.

In the midst of this need, some boys struggle to bond with other boys. They long for a sense of belonging, but may feel alienated, isolated, left out, rejected, put to the side, and not a part of the group. They can experience "estrangement" from same-sex peers, which is simply another form of detachment. Feelings of estrangement are often due to the behavior of other boys. A young man naturally wants to be liked, appreciated, and accepted by the group. He wants to spend time talking, sharing, and hanging out—to be a part of the crew. He hopes to bond and feel wanted by same-sex peers. He's looking for real love that is freely offered by other boys.[22] One author suggested that "men need other men for support when the situation seems more than hopeless. We need someone to drag us out of the jungle when we've had our legs [injured] by the landmines of life."[23]

A good example of male connection is illustrated in the movie *The Sandlot*. The boys have a campout, eat s'mores, tell ghost stories, tease each other, share secrets, talk about girls, and have great adventures together. Boys seek adventure with each other. It's interesting that some psychologists have noted how boys show love through

---

21 Flores, P. J. (2012). *Addiction as an attachment disorder*. Lanham: Jason Aronson, p.218.

22 Baer, G. (2003). *Real love: The truth about finding unconditional love and fulfilling relationships*. New York: Gotham Books, p. 45.

23 Dusek, D. (2015). *Rough Cut Men - A Man's Battle Guide to Building Real Relationships with Each Other and with Jesus*. Issaquah, WA: Made For Success Publishing, p.36.

---

action. A boy is more likely to desire bonding through activity than simple talking.[24]

Similarly, boys often physically compete with one another and create friendships from the experience. Competition becomes a form of nurturing – a way to lift each other up, support each other, and work together in a team. They grow together through competition and teamwork. Unfortunately, a boy on the sidelines is going to be overlooked and less likely to be invited into the circle.[25]

The desire for same-sex connection seems obvious. Again, *The Sandlot* creates a fantastic illustration. It depicts the father-hunger of a boy who becomes engulfed by the protection and love of young men in the neighborhood. "No man is designed to travel alone or battle without covering fire. And no man is truly safe without authentic friendship."[26] The absence of these attachment opportunities creates estrangement, and the attachment longings persist.

A good explanation of estrangement comes from a gay author who cringes from the memory of being taunted. Other boys called him sissy and faggot long before any of them knew what it meant. All he knew was that it was something unspeakable and that other boys thought he was loathsome. Unfortunately, boys who detach have internalized the names they were called during moments of teasing and taunting. The labels become a stake driven into their heart and toxic to the soul. To be called a sissy or wimp is anything but positive and affirming.[27]

Have you ever heard the expression, "Sticks and stones may break my bones, but names will never hurt me?" In my case, and for others like me, the names were more painful than sticks or stones. The scrapes and bruises left by real sticks and stones heal more easily than emotional wounds created by rejection, teasing, and

---

24 Pollack, W. S. (1999). *Real boys: Rescuing our sons from the myths of boyhood.* New York: Henry Holt and Company, p. 66.

25 Gurian, M. (2006). *The wonder of boys: What parents, mentors and educators to do to shape boys into exceptional men.* New York: Jeremy P. Tarcher/Penguin, p. 29.

26 Dusek, D. (2015), p47.

27 Crawford, D. (1998). *Easing the ache: Gay men recovering from compulsive behaviors.* Center City, Minn: Hazelden.

---

taunting. "Rejection is a wound that is created when those around us deliver a clear signal, whether intentional or unintentional, that we are not good enough, that we are not wanted, that we are not valued, or that we don't belong."[28]

As a young man, I looked for approval from boys my age. I experienced name-calling and labeling that was painful. I was called a wimp. I was deflated and pushed away by other boys. Even the boys at church (a place where one should feel loved and accepted) left me out. Rather than feeling like one of the guys, I felt like an outcast. The sense of general rejection was strong and the dream of having buddies seemed beyond my reach.

To cope, I created a simple pattern of avoidance; I stopped trying to connect with them in any meaningful way. This reinforced my sense of loneliness and estrangement. I didn't want to play with them because my feelings were hurt. It was a double-bind: I wanted to interact but believed I would be rejected. It felt like I would lose either way. It was almost as though I had one foot on the brake pedal and one foot on the gas pedal at the same time. I was spinning my wheels but not moving.

I isolated myself both physically and emotionally. I avoided guys at school as often as possible. I hung out with girls who were nice to me. I continued to tell myself, *"I don't care what the boys say,"* though deep inside I really did care.

During high school, my family moved to a small town of cowboys and farmers. I tried to fit in, but it was a culture shock. Core emotions like sadness, fear, and anger – which I didn't know how to express – became intense. My social anxiety escalated, which further estranged me from other young men. Particularly at school, the kids didn't seem to want me there. I felt different and unwelcome. I was the big-city kid trying to fit in with the small-town kids. There was no sense of belonging to the group.

One day while sitting in class the teacher stood up and momentarily left the room. As the door closed, a rowdy group of teens threw erasers from the chalkboard at me. The teacher returned to the room as I sat in a cloud of chalk. I was embarrassed and angry, but I bottled the emotions up like a pressure cooker. The cowboy kids seemed to feel the need to put me in my place. I was the trendy teenager with stylish clothes and a haircut, which made me an easy target in this small town. I was frequently invited to fight after school with boys I hadn't ever met. This caused my fear and anxiety to increase, and I went out of my way to avoid confrontation. Without any outlet for my emotions, I simply swallowed the feelings. As I look back, I can see that

---

28 Love, T. L. (2017). *Finding Peace - A Workbook on Healing from Loss, Neglect, Rejection, Abandonment, Betrayal and Abuse.* Yuma, AZ: Love and Light Publishing, p. 15.

I might have placed myself in situations that made it more difficult to fit in, but the feelings of rejection and detachment were intense.

Here is the important takeaway: When a boy feels a sense of estrangement, he may begin to ignore his need for attachment. He isn't bonding and detaches from male peers. He may start to pretend he doesn't care and try to bury the legitimate need.

Attachment needs cannot be overlooked

However, the desire to be loved and accepted by other boys and men is an important part of growing up. The attachment needs cannot be overlooked. This is a natural longing that doesn't just disappear. All boys have an intrinsic need to relate and bond with one another. They want to belong and feel like "one of the guys." During periods of social development, when there is no healthy outlet for expressing core emotion, these unmet attachment drives can become sexualized.

One of the reasons that group therapy is so helpful for sexualized attachments is due to the ongoing need for connection. The legitimate needs are satisfied through healthy intimacy. Alexandra Katehakis commented that most individuals in recovery for sexual addiction improve faster in group therapy because our brains are social organs, requiring a community for growth and healing.[29]

---

29 Katehakis, A. (2016). Sex addiction as affect dysregulation: A neurobiologically informed holistic treatment. New York: W. W. Norton & company, p. 225.

Chapter 9 Questions

1. Which words below best describe any estrangement you experienced?

❑ Isolated   ❑ Taunted   ❑ Rejected   ❑ Unappreciated

❑ Teased   ❑ Forgotten   ❑ Alienated   ❑ Abandoned

❑ Ignore   ❑ Left out   ❑ Abused   ❑ Brushed off

❑ Alone   ❑ Criticized   ❑ Beat Up   ❑ Overlooked

2. Write in detail about what this estrangement is like for you.

_____

_____

_____

_____

_____

3. Write about a time you felt detached or estranged from male peers.

_____

_____

_____

_____

_____

4. In what way do you most often disconnect from guys?

_____

_____

_____

_____

5. Are there ways that you cause estrangement?

_____

_____

_____

_____

_____

6. Write about a time you felt estranged or detached from male peers and noticed a strong desire for their attention or affection.

_____

_____

_____

_____

_____

7. Which core emotions did you experience as a child: Fear? Sadness? Anger? Please describe.

_____

_____

_____

_____

_____

_____

_____

_____

_____

Chapter 10

Gender Congruency
Perceptions of Masculinity

Most parents strive to help their children feel good about themselves and confident as unique individuals. However, kids must consider whether they feel masculine as a boy or feminine as a girl. When a boy grows to feel inherently masculine, or a girl to feel inherently feminine, the child develops a sense of gender congruency. In other words, the way they view themselves is congruent with their own *perception* of what is either masculine or feminine. This concept of congruence contributes to the child's sense of gender identity, which is essentially their innate sense of themselves.

Gender congruency is not a moral issue. It is simply the comparison of what the child perceives as masculine or feminine against their own perception of themselves. To be gender congruent would mean that the child's perception of masculine or feminine, is completely in line (congruent) with how they see themselves. In other words, their perception of what is culturally expected matches their own perception of who they are as a boy or girl. If their perception of masculinity or femininity seems different than how they see themselves, they feel gender *in*congruent.

Gender congruency is often influenced by cultural norms and attachment issues. Additionally, there are varying degrees of congruence as no one is 100% congruent with perceptions of themselves as completely masculine or feminine. Interestingly, I've observed countless adults with pronounced incongruency who also report stronger attachment problems.

Boys develop confidence about their own masculinity as they grow and test themselves alongside other boys and men. They come to see themselves as competent in the world of men. Different cultures have differing norms about masculine and feminine behavior. In some cultures, boys test themselves in athletics, academics, scouting, mechanics, or other areas to achieve a sense of confidence. They look for opportunities to prove to themselves that they are "competent."

Initiation rites marking the passage of a boy into manhood have been maintained by some cultures, notably the African Maasai, the American Lakota, the ancient Romans, and the Jewish people.[30] Unfortunately, these rites of passage don't exist in various industrialized nations like the United States. Boys are often left to search for answers on their own. "They are confused, hurting and feeling terribly incomplete. They rarely learn from the adults closest to them what it means to become a man – or learn when they have become one."[31]

A boy may have an awareness of his body parts that make him male but, unfortunately, perceives himself as less than what's expected by his culture. He desires to be like the other boys but doesn't feel like he measures up – a sense that he doesn't belong to the tribe. If he begins to separate himself from other boys his personal sense of inadequacy strengthens gender incongruence.

A gay author once commented that he remembers being the last one picked for teams, teased for throwing like a girl, and the focus of jokes during active games. He dreaded gym class and the locker room. He felt wholly inadequate in front of the other boys and always felt they were making a fool of him.[32] His personal sense of incongruence was intense.

In many cases the sense of incongruence is quietly hidden by an embarrassed, deflated, or confused boy. But sometimes, gender becomes more obvious if he displays effeminate or girlish characteristics. This young man does not resonate with masculine qualities. He might even develop a distaste for what maleness represents. In addition, he may avoid certain male activities because he does not understand them or because he's anxious about them.

Emotional wounds from sports and athletics can be a common experience that creates insecurity. The wounds will skew their sense of how to fit into the world of boys and men. They might compare themselves with others when they cannot perform at the same level. Being teased, ridiculed, or the last one picked for a team can weaken their sense of confidence. One psychiatrist observed that sports-wounds negatively affect a boy's image of himself and his confidence in the world of boys and men. It impacts his friendships, his gender identity, and his body image. His negative perception of himself, and his need for attachment, can lead him to crave the

---

30 Molitor, B. D. (2001). *A Boy's Passage - Celebrating Your Son's Journey to Maturity*. Colorado Springs, CO: WaterBrook Press, pp. 1-16.

31 Molitor, B.D. (2001), p. 23.

32 Crawford, D. (1998). *Easing the Ache: Gay men recovering from compulsive behaviors*. Center City, Minn: Hazelden.

masculinity of his male peers.[33] Another author observed a client was strongly drawn toward other men when he felt overwhelmed or inadequate.[34]

Similarly, psychologists Hockenberry and Bingham discovered that through modeling experiences with one another boys learned behaviors that encouraged healthy identity and personal sense of masculinity.[35] In other words, it seemed to be a *learned* confidence.

As I started working with a counselor to find healing, I realized that as a child I had been fearful of injury, avoided physical fights, played more with girls, and described myself as an occasional loner who seldom played boys' competitive games. These traits prevented me from healthy and common boyhood interactions that generate a sense of strength, masculinity, and gender congruency. I was experiencing gender incongruence at a young age. Somehow, I just felt less legitimate than my peers.

One of my adult clients said it this way: *"I watched other boys play and longed to be skillful and athletic. The boys around me seemed further ahead, more coordinated, and athletic. I hadn't learned to play team sports. I didn't understand the rough games and horseplay. I certainly didn't see games as a form of male bonding. I didn't know how to do the things I instinctively believed were masculine. Common tasks and activities in which boys engaged were foreign to me. I was not a part of their world. I felt inadequate as a male. I desperately wanted to feel masculine and confident."*

---

33 Fitzgibbons, R., MD. (n.d.). Library: The Origins and Healing of Homosexual Attractions. Retrieved July 28, 2018, https://www.catholicculture.org/culture/library/view.cfm?id=3112.

34 Ethridge, S. (2012). *The Fantasy fallacy: Exposing the deeper meaning behind sexual thoughts*. Waterville, Me.: Christian Large Print Originals, p. 135.

35 Hockenberry, S. L., & Billingham, R. E. (1988). Sexual orientation and boyhood gender conformity: Development of the Boyhood Gender Conformity Scale (BGCS). *Archives of Sexual Behavior*,17(3), 287-287. doi:10.1007/bf01541748

Chapter 10 Questions

1. Gender congruence is when a person's _____ of what is expected to be masculine, matches the perception of _____.

2. What qualities do you perceive as masculine? Write others not listed.

❑ Athletic   ❑ Smart   ❑ Confident   ❑ Mechanical

❑ Outgoing   ❑ Muscular   ❑ Sporty   ❑ Well-dressed

❑ Funny   ❑ Social   ❑ Academic   ❑ Strong

❑ Other _____

❑ Other _____

❑ Other _____

❑ Other _____

❑ Other _____

3. What are the qualities you feel are not masculine about yourself?

_____

_____

_____

_____

_____

_____

_____

_____

_____

_____

_____

_____

4. What masculine qualities do you most envy about other boys or men?

_____

_____

_____

_____

_____

_____

_____

_____

5. Write about a time when you felt less masculine and compared yourself to other boys/men.

_____

_____

_____

_____

_____

_____

_____

_____

_____

6. Write about a time you felt envy for other boys' masculine qualities.

_____

_____

_____

_____

_____

_____

_____

_____

_____

_____

_____

_____

_____

_____

_____

_____

_____

_____

_____

_____

_____

_____

Chapter 11

Emotional Preoccupation

Difficulties and wounds are common in the search for connection. For some boys it becomes a serious struggle to attach in healthy ways. Sometimes a young man with sexualized attachments may have been detached from his father. He might feel disconnected and estranged from other boys. Feelings of inferiority might cause him to dwell on thoughts about boys and masculine traits. The attachment struggle creates a whirlwind of feelings and he develops an emotional preoccupation.

The emotional preoccupation is composed of thoughts and feelings caused by attachment deficits and wounds. Examples might include jealousy, envy, fear, anxiety, rumination, daydreams, idolization, comparisons, or curiosity. The emotional preoccupation becomes an internal pressure.

As a boy develops, his body manufactures hormones that produce sexual urges. This is natural and normal. It's also new and exciting. Every young man will experience growing curiosity about sexuality. The curiosity increases as he matures so never shame yourself for having sexual urges; they are not bad. These feelings are a natural part of human experience; they are good.

However, when a young man is emotionally preoccupied with other boys or masculinity, while at the same time his sexual urges are growing, the impulses will be drawn together. Essentially, the emotional intensity draws the sexual urge like magnetism and they become intertwined. The longer this continues the deeper the imprinting. Over time, sexual impulse occurs whenever emotional preoccupation rises. It becomes automatic and feels as though it has always been that way. Some will say it feels natural. Eventually it will be hard to distinguish what is sexual and what is emotional because they are so intricately connected.

At this point an arousal pattern develops and the boy's sexual urges become interwoven with emotion. As the pattern is strengthened over time it becomes imprinted and forms an arousal template. He might have attachment needs for love and attention from other men or boys, but now the drive toward attachment becomes a sexual desire. The unfulfilled need for bonding presents itself with sexual energy.

Jealousy & Envy

Most boys find themselves admiring young men for various traits and features. This is normal. They quietly watch and think: *"I wish I was popular like him,"* or *"I wish my body was muscular like his,"* or *"If only I could play sports as well as he does."* These thoughts of jealousy or envy are common. Although most young men will experience jealousy, most are not feeling the same level of intensity about it as a young man with attachment wounds. Why is that? Because most boys generally feel they belong – that they are "one of the guys." They don't feel overly anxious or inadequate about doing male things.

Another one of my close friends in recovery said, *"All I ever wanted was to belong. I wanted to play ball and not feel like a wimp. To joke around and have fun with buddies. I wanted to feel like a regular guy. But instead, I just watched and admired them. I was filled with envy and desire to be like them. I wanted to fit in, be approved, and welcomed by them. A tremendous amount of envy, jealousy, rejection, and longing sprang up in its place."*

Just like my friend, I remember watching boys in the locker room and feeling jealous about their bodies. I wanted mine to be more like theirs. When I sat in class, I watched other boys joke around. I wanted so much to be funny and popular like them. I envied their friendships. I wanted to belong to the group. When at church, I watched them play basketball and wished I could play well. I wanted to be included and feel athletically confident. I generally sat on the sidelines and allowed jealousy and envy to occupy my mind. I was usually filled with social anxiety so, rather than learn how to play or socialize, I just sat on the sidelines and let my thoughts consume me. Envious energy permeated my soul. I frequently told myself, *"I'm just not like other guys. I'm different."*

Fear & Anxiety

Fear pressures humans to keep safe and avoid risk. Frequently, we hide our fears from others. Keeping fear trapped inside only magnifies the energy and our fears grow into anxiety.

I remember visiting with a young man who had attachment wounds with peers. His parents signed him up for Boy Scouts but he told me he felt superior to the guys in his Troop. He also explained that he didn't like Scouting and found it to be a waste of time. However, his stated goal of therapy was to regain connection with other young men so I suggested he engage the opportunity with scouting. He turned to me and said, *"I told you I don't like Scouting and it's a waste of my time."*

I continued to encourage him that it doesn't hurt to try new things. After all, he was asking my help to make connections with his peers. I suggested he might find it to be a good experience if he surrendered his judgments. In an irritated tone he continued, *"You can't make me go. I don't like it!"* His tone had escalated and seemed a bit panicked. I was surprised by his reaction, so I asked him to tell me more. He teared up, hung his head, and revealed his fear of rejection and embarrassment.

Later, he admitted that his response was an anxious reaction. He was deeply afraid of more rejection. He didn't want others to see him as weak or incompetent. He wanted to fit in with these boys, not to be an outcast. He buried his fears rather than confronting them and developed anxiety about scouting.

I worked with another young man who acted self-righteous around other boys. He would lecture them whenever they talked about girls in romantic or curious ways. He would say, *"Women shouldn't be treated as objects."* He told them it was wrong and they should value girls for who they are. He continued by saying that it was ungodly to focus on a woman's appearance. His lectures came across as conceited and arrogant and, as a result, the other boys pulled away from him. They were sharing natural curiosity about girls not harassing or objectifying them. But his fear of sin and looking inept created anxiety. This anxiety caused him to distance himself from boys and their light-hearted conversations about girls. He sacrificed friendships and male bonding that he deeply needed.

In some cases, a young man develops clinical anxiety. This condition creates an obstacle for bonding and attachment. It involves incessant worry and rumination that eventually causes physical symptoms: headaches, stomachaches, body-aches, diarrhea, or other ailments. General unease, phobias, or obsessive-compulsive tendencies can make social interaction awkward and uncomfortable. Specific phobias might develop toward activities that boys often do together such as sports. A young man could

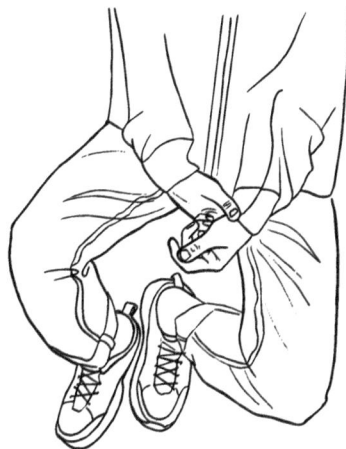

feel anxious and cannot relax sufficiently to bond with others. In this case, therapy to diminish anxiety issues and learn healthy social skills will be necessary.

Rumination and Negativity

Ruminating on something means that you are dwelling on it. I allowed myself to harbor resentment and anger toward my father and others who I perceived had rejected me. I filled my mind with cussing and images of retaliation. Although my father sometimes apologized, I would respond in my mind: *"It doesn't matter what you say. I still hate you!"* I never said this out loud, but thought about it. Likewise, I harbored anger toward other boys who left me out, teased, or bullied me.

Consumed by resentment, I focused on my own imperfections. I refused to see my own positive qualities or achievements. I fixated on thoughts of inadequacy. If I lagged behind during P.E. I would think about it all day long. I centered my thoughts on personal failure and overlooked success. It didn't matter that I was now popular, musical, a Sterling Scholar, an Eagle Scout, and Captain of the swim team, because I let my failures overshadow my successes. I was skilled at rumination – focusing on the negative about myself and others.

Daydreams

When I wasn't in school, I spent time thinking about guys and reminding myself of my own inadequacies. *"If I was like that guy then everyone would like me,"* or *"I can't stand myself because my body is not developed and muscular like that guy,"* or *"He would hang out with me if I didn't stink at softball,"* or *"If I wasn't such a loser, I'd have a group of close buddies."*

I could bring vivid images into my mind about idealized characteristics I was lacking in myself. I used to imagine myself as a popular star athlete. I imagined moments of glory in sports. I envisioned sharing good times with a best friend. These daydreams filled my mind and created further discontent. It's almost as though I was daydreaming about the resolution of my attachment needs and wounds.

Idolization

Sometimes I took jealousy to higher levels, placing other young men on a pedestal. My attachment wounds caused me to idolize other boys. I ranked them as larger than life. The qualities and traits I admired became paramount. In my mind, I perceived other young men as superior to myself; as innately better than me. I focused on the admirable qualities they possessed while minimizing my own. I positioned these young men in my heart as more important and valuable.

As a teenager, I remember looking through clothing catalogs and feeling drawn to the stylish attire. Most of the young men in the pictures were attractive and physically developed, smiling, and confident. I wanted to be the boys in the photos: confident, athletic, happy, and playful. These were the traits which I idolized.

A couple of friends that I met in my addiction recovery program helped me to see this more clearly. The first friend was Alan who described a longing for masculine contact he never received in childhood. He wanted connection in every way with those he perceived as truly masculine. He said this longing became an idolization of boys that held certain qualities.

The second friend, Rich, said he felt deficient as a male and yearned to be accepted and affirmed by those whose masculinity he admired the most. He began to idolize the qualities in other males that he judged to be lacking in himself. He also put them on a pedestal that glorified them and made them unapproachable, which in turn magnified his whole dilemma.

Comparisons

Once I started idolizing same-sex peers, I started to view myself as inferior to them in different ways; I compared myself. Boys with attachment wounds frequently make unfair comparisons. They take ideal qualities in other young men and compare those qualities to imperfections and lesser qualities in themselves. It often becomes difficult to avoid comparisons. The traits a young man believes he is lacking get compared to idolized traits of other boys. This is totally unfair to himself.

I compared everything. I thought I was not as athletic as the other boys (although I was captain of the swim team), I saw myself as skinny and small (although I was muscular and cut from swimming), I perceived that I was never funny (although friends laughed at my jokes), I believed I was never as popular (although I was nominated in high school for "Man of the Year"). I was constantly pounding myself down and grew mentally exhausted from unrelenting comparisons.

Curiosity

I didn't understand other boys and was comparing myself incessantly. I couldn't relate to them. They became intriguing in a new way. I was curious about how they were thinking and why they would act the way they did. Furthermore, I didn't know how to get answers. I realized later that boys resolve curiosity by simply asking questions, talking, and interacting. I missed those opportunities because I pulled away. I didn't have any enduring attachment to any one buddy with whom I could discuss life-questions or challenges.

Changes during puberty also puzzled me. I didn't understand what was happening to my body. I was inhibited talking with other boys about it and left curious about the changes happening to them. I was insecure and unsettled. These exciting but strange changes left me without answers.

I realized later that I had missed common experiences that give boys opportunities to talk, interact, and resolve curiosity. For example, changing or showering in the locker room provides a chance to banter and joke with one another. It gives them a natural outlet to see each other's body and resolve any mystery. There will be conversations about school, girls, parents, sex, sports, teachers, and puberty. Although the talk may be crude at times, any joking or teasing is often an attempt to connect. Unfortunately, my own fear and anxiety caused me to withdraw from these natural opportunities.

Chapter 11 Questions

1. Essentially, the emotional intensity draws the _____ urge like a magnet, and they become intertwined. The longer this happens, the deeper the _____ becomes.

2. List any boys for whom you feel jealous or envious.

_____

_____

_____

3. List qualities or traits of boys that make you jealous or envious.

_____

_____

_____

_____

_____

_____

4. How do you feel about yourself regarding those qualities or traits?

_____

_____

_____

_____

_____

_____

_____

5. Write about a time when your jealousy and envy were strong, and you noticed it became sexualized.

_____

_____

_____

_____

_____

_____

_____

6. Write about interactions that may cause you fear or anxiety.

_____

_____

_____

_____

_____

7. In what ways do you ruminate – harbor negativity?

❑ I hold grudges   ❑ I refuse to let go of the past

❑ I tease   ❑ I point out other boys' weaknesses

❑ I don't forgive   ❑ I focus on my bad qualities

❑ I treat others rudely   ❑ I beat myself up inside

❑ I gossip about others   ❑ I remind myself of my failures

❑ Other _____

❑ Other _____

8. Describe how you think your own negativity has impacted you.

_____

_____

_____

_____

_____

_____

_____

9. Describe a daydream you've had about other boys or men. Be specific. Include names of people, the place it occurs, and the details of what happens.

_____

_____

_____

_____

_____

_____

_____

_____

_____

10. List boys or men that you idolize.

_____

_____

_____

_____

11. List the qualities these boys or men have that you idolize in them.

_____

_____

_____

_____

_____

_____

_____

12. What comparisons do you make between yourself and others?

_____

_____

_____

_____

_____

_____

_____

13. What personal inadequacies do you focus on?

_____

_____

_____

_____

_____

_____

_____

14. Do you ever feel curious about boys/men in the following ways?

❑ Why other boys/men talk the way they do.

❑ Why boys/men enjoy certain games and activities.

❑ What other boys/men talk about with each other.

❑ Other boys'/men's bodies.

❑ How my body compares to other boys/men.

❑ How other boys/men work through problems.

❑ How boys/men show affection for each other.

❑ Puberty and how it affects other boys.

❑ How boys/men think.

❑ What other boys/men are thinking and feeling.

❑ How other boys/men overcome fear.

❑ Other _____

❑ Other _____

15. What keeps you from resolving curiosities?

_____

_____

_____

_____

_____

_____

_____

_____

_____

_____

_____

_____

16. Is there anything else about boys, men, or masculinity that emotionally consumes your thoughts?

_____

_____

_____

_____

_____

_____

_____

_____

_____

_____

_____

_____

Chapter 12

Attachment with Opposite-Sex Peers

Some boys are confused about their relationship with the opposite sex and develop emotional blocks. These blocks are related to attachment needs, so a young man may need to address these various blocks which hinder healthy interaction with girls.

Over-Identification

Some boys will over-identify with girls. At a time when most boys develop a deeper connection with buddies, I felt safer and more comfortable around girls as friends and sisters. It was easier to relate and socialize with them. My comfort around girls turned into an over-identification with them. I couldn't see them as dating or romantic partners. This over-identification blocked me from healthy romantic interest and curiosity.

In my world girls felt safer even though they were sometimes emotional, so I chose to associate mostly with them. They didn't play rough. They liked to talk. They cared about my feelings. I felt closer to girls than to boys. I played with them during recess in elementary school. In high school, my closest friends were girls. I was identifying myself more with women than with men. Girls were like sisters; it just felt wrong to think of them romantically. On one hand I felt closer to girls, and on the other I felt disgusted by romance with them.

Masculine Negativity

When I was a child, I fondly remember my aunt and grandmother coming to visit. While I was close to these loving women in my life, I could often sense their negative opinion about men. I heard my grandmother and aunt commiserate about how men never understand or listen and that they were generally abusive and controlling. I was hearing a message about men as bad and unworthy, and my own father's behavior reinforced this imagery. He was often rude and calloused, rarely listened, and was generally controlling. Who wants to bond with the bad guy? The negative message caused me to push further away from my dad. I didn't feel like I belonged to the world of men; a fraternity that seemed unsafe and unwelcoming.

As I matured, I didn't want to be like my father, but also didn't appreciate the harsh commentary against my own gender. It was a double-bind. I was a boy after all! I started to see some women as negative and manipulative. I began to dislike any feminine hostility displayed against men. I perceived negative comments as unnecessary and dramatic.

Feminine Abuse

In fifth grade, I was visiting some friends when one of the older sisters coaxed me into her bedroom. I didn't want to be there but didn't want to make her mad. She pressured me to make-out with her — a manipulated experience that swept away any curiosity. I didn't like her physical advances and felt coerced and controlled. This girl was neither playful nor fun, and the emotion while kissing was not enjoyable.

On another occasion, two older and very assertive junior high girls cornered me in the hallway. When no one was around, they held me against the wall and groped me. I was humiliated and scanned the area to make sure no other boys had seen it happen. A girl had challenged my masculinity and I had lost; I felt weak. I wanted to be strong and defend myself, but I had allowed girls to touch me in private places. How could I let this happen? I never told anyone about the experience and it reinforced my belief that girls could be abusive. I found myself avoiding romantic possibilities. Ultimately, manipulation and abuse from girls blocked me from viewing them as romantic partners.

Moral Anxiety

My sensitive nature made me prone to general anxiety and during high school I found myself seeking medication to cope. I started getting stomach aches and headaches and often couldn't sleep at night. This general anxiety spilled over into my religious beliefs, and moral anxiety became another block to romantic curiosity. In his research, Dr. Jeff Robinson observed various blocks that often prevented his clients from connecting with the opposite sex in romantic ways.[36] Among these blocks was moral anxiety. Moral anxiety is when a young man feels anxious about "sinful" behavior with girls and simply cannot see girls in romantic ways – he wants to do the "right" thing.

I wanted to please God and was afraid of doing something wrong or sinful. I was taught that girls should be respected and that I should deny myself anything romantic or sexual; that these desires were wrong and sinful.

One Sunday in church our family sat down in our regular pew. We happened to sit next to another family with an attractive teenage girl my age. She smiled at me and we sat right next to each other. My father was so perturbed about the seating arrangement that he got up during the service and moved himself between us. I was embarrassed by his response and was sure everyone in church had noticed. His behavior sent a negative message about flirting and my anxiety became further entrenched.

While in high school I attended church camp. As we were boarding the bus, I sat down with one of the guys in my group. During our light conversation he turned quietly and asked me if there was a girl I'd like to kiss. His casual curiosity dumbfounded me. In shock I asked myself, *"How could another Christian ask such a thing?"* I held onto an anxious belief that romantic and sexual activity should wait until marriage. I labeled this other boy as sinful and pulled away from his friendship. The anxiety I felt about a romantic relationship with any girl created a huge block. I could not even allow myself to be curious.

36 Robinson, J., Dr. (n.d.). Understanding Unwanted Same-Sex Attraction. Retrieved August 10, 2018, from http://www.theguardrail.com/

Performance Anxiety

Another emotional block identified by Dr. Robinson is performance anxiety.[37] This is the worry and tension a young man feels about his ability to "perform" romantically with a girl; he's just not sure he can get aroused or that he will know the right things to do with a girl. According to Robinson, this block can also inhibit a young man from learning romantic interaction with the opposite sex.

I certainly didn't know how to date or interact with girls in ways that were not friendship-oriented. I tried dating and found myself awkward and uncertain. Throughout high school I attempted to connect romantically, but finally gave up as it was too uncomfortable and unfamiliar.

In summary, how a boy learns to connect and relate to the opposite sex can present challenges. He may develop an over-identification with girls and fail to see them with any romantic possibility. He may also develop blocks that inhibit natural curiosity or dating skills. Furthermore, he may experience various forms of abuse that create blocks toward women. If a young man is confused about his attachment with women, it will create unseen obstacles to healthy development.

---

37 Robinson, J., Dr. (n.d.). Understanding Unwanted Same-Sex Attraction. Retrieved August 10, 2018, from http://www.theguardrail.com/

Chapter 12 Questions

1. Mark any perceptions you have of girls:

❑ Harsh   ❑ Absent   ❑ Soft   ❑ Caring

❑ Strong   ❑ Sensitive   ❑ Abrupt   ❑ Domineering

❑ Weak   ❑ Helpful   ❑ Friendly   ❑ Controlling

❑ Gentle   ❑ Critical   ❑ Positive   ❑ Smothering

2. What blocks have you developed with girls?

_____

_____

_____

_____

3. In what ways have you over-identified with girls?

_____

_____

_____

_____

_____

4. What blocks prevent you from connecting with girls romantically?

_____

_____

_____

_____

_____

5. How do these blocks prevent you from connecting romantically?

_____

_____

_____

_____

_____

_____

_____

6. Have you developed unhealthy connections with girls?

_____

_____

_____

_____

_____

7. How does this prevent you from connecting with girls romantically?

_____

_____

_____

_____

_____

_____

Chapter 13

Body Issues

Unsettled concerns or insecurity about his body can diminish a young man's confidence; he may feel inferior or self-conscious. Issues about his body can make his attachment efforts more difficult. He might even block healthy opportunities for connection.

I was skinny and awkward. I avoided rough, team activities and was not encouraged to participate in sports. When I watched other boys compete, my mind was filled with comparisons against myself. I was insecure about my body. When changing in the locker room or taking showers after PE, the comparisons were impossible to ignore. Other young men had body hair in places that I did not. They were often taller and more muscular. I was younger, shorter, skinnier, and less developed.

Moral anxiety contributed to the insecurity because I was worried about making the right choices. I was very anxious about displeasing God. I didn't want to be immodest so undressing in the locker room was not only awkward, but felt wrong. The other boys would undress and change without hesitation. I felt guilty as well as insecure about anyone seeing me. These anxieties and fears inhibited me and, in some instances, paralyzed me.

My insecurity caused me to withdraw and become extremely modest. I was afraid to take my shirt off in front of other boys. Playing shirts-and-skins for basketball struck panic inside me. I was terrified to take a shower after gym and have the boys look at me. I remember listening to them joke around in the shower. I wanted to be a part of the group but wouldn't risk the vulnerability. I was stunned they could be so casual chatting about the day while taking a shower. It didn't seem to bother them at all. They held a confidence that I didn't possess.

Negative body image affects a boy's self-esteem and can make it difficult for him to engage attachment opportunities. During sixth grade, my teeth became a social obstacle for me. They were terribly crooked and in junior high I didn't smile. Fortunately, my parents had the foresight to get me braces. Having straight teeth raised my confidence and I was more willing to try and socialize.

Some boys with acne will avoid social events. I remember a young man who had problems with his feet which made it hard for him to run and participate in athletic events. Various physical issues that can perpetuate a loss in confidence can be addressed with professional help. When possible, body issues should be confronted. Get some help. Don't make life harder than it needs to be.

One of my colleagues observed that body-image wounds seem to be high for young men with attachment issues. These young men often feel a lower sense of self-worth due to feelings of inadequacy about their appearance. They detach from their own body as it reminds them of their own perceived inferiority.

Identifying issues you may have about your body will be important so you can make changes. These issues may directly impact other areas of healing as they relate to confidence, social interaction, sporting activities, etc. You may need to resolve body issues to increase your confidence and resolve attachment issues.

Chapter 13 Questions

1. Are there things about your body that make you feel insecure?

_____

_____

_____

_____

_____

_____

_____

_____

_____

_____

_____

2. What would you like to change about your body?

_____

_____

_____

_____

_____

_____

_____

_____

3. Write about a time when your insecurities prevented you from activities with male peers?

_____

_____

_____

_____

_____

_____

_____

_____

_____

_____

_____

_____

_____

_____

_____

_____

_____

_____

_____

Chapter 14

Attachment and Affection

When a sense of safety and attachment has been established in a relationship, healthy affection comes naturally. It seems to strengthen bonding and connection. In other words, the relationship feels more grounded and secure.

This need for affection is hard-wired into us from birth. Parents will hold their infants as a primary way to offer love and security.[38] There may be times when a young man is starved for physical affection from other boys or mentors. This feeling can easily become sexualized if not received in a healthy manner.

I watched boys at school show affection for one another and was filled with envy. I desperately wanted the camaraderie they shared. They seemed at ease with physical affection and banter. They walked together pushing and being playful. At church they would greet one another with a hug. I watched them slap each other on the back during basketball. There was never anything sexual about it. I found myself physically yearning for this contact.

My father was rarely affectionate with me and when he tried it was awkward for us both. I've talked to countless other young men with sexualized attachments who report the same experience with their fathers.

After a semester of college, one of my roommates named Glenn was preparing to go home. He wouldn't be returning to college, so we would be looking for a new housemate. We had spent nights studying together and laughing. He was playful and easygoing. I was connecting with Glenn and his departure would leave a void inside me.

---

38 Mooney, C. G. (2010). *Theories of attachment: An introduction to Bowlby, Ainsworth, Gerber, Brazelton, Kennell, and Klaus.* St. Paul, MN: Redleaf Press, p. 88.

I helped him load his luggage into his car and he surprised me with a bearhug. I hadn't expected this token of friendship. He didn't let go and I became emotional. I'd never experienced this before. He started to cry while he hugged me and told me how much he loved me. He reminded me about the good times we had together. Now I was crying. We were truly friends, and he was going to miss me. This token of love and affection filled my hungry soul. I realized how starved I had been for this type of contact. It was this masculine love between two brothers that I had never before experienced.

At this moment, I realized that my lack of affectionate touch with other boys and men had been unhealthy. Over time I developed other friendships that were equally affectionate. I learned that men generally have a common desire for affection with each other. I started paying more attention to men at church when they would hug each other. In youth ministry I noticed boys putting their arms around each other to pray for one another. It appeared natural, not forced.

This new revelation started shifting the moral anxiety I had developed. I realized: *"Maybe God knows I need affection and doesn't see it as sinful. In fact, maybe God wired me to be affectionate. Which then means it would be important to learn how to give and receive it from other men."*

As I read through my Bible, I noticed numerous examples of affection by spiritual men and women. This was especially true about stories of healing. Once when Jesus was traveling with his disciples, he stopped to heal a blind man. "They came to Bethsaida, and some people brought a blind man and begged Jesus to <u>touch</u> him. He <u>took the blind man by the hand</u> and <u>led him</u> outside the village. When he had spit on the man's eyes and <u>put his hands on him</u>, Jesus asked, 'Do you see anything?' He looked up and said, 'I see people; they look like trees walking around.' Once more Jesus <u>put his hands on the man's eyes</u>. Then his eyes were opened, his sight was restored, and he saw everything clearly."[39]

Why would God literally touch the man? Why would this be necessary for an

---

39 Mark 8:22-26, NIV

all-powerful God? Perhaps the answer is more about our human need for physical contact. He wanted to connect with those he was healing. He knows we need this. He wired us this way. Affection is healing and essential for healthy attachment. God knows it, and He knows we need it.

An interesting article by Dr. Benjamin describes the death of babies in orphanages at the turn of the century. Unwanted infants were often delivered to orphanages where sterile procedures and sufficient food seemed to guarantee an opportunity for life. But these babies often died. The access to food, water, and shelter didn't seem to matter.

Ultimately, they concluded that these babies died from lack of physical nurture and affection. This was the only missing possibility. When babies were switched to new orphanages where they received physical affection and nurturing care, they gained weight and began to thrive.[40]

North American culture has made it difficult for men to express affection. An interesting article that describes the disintegration of healthy affection between boys and men was written by Brett and Kate McKay. They describe how modern American culture has caused men to be cautious - to avoid sending the message they are gay. McKay believes this is the reason men have become less comfortable expressing affection with one another.[41] They also describe other cultures where it appears common for men to be affectionate with one another and comfortable with things like holding hands.[42] Through a series of historical photographs, they depict men showing healthy affection before everyone was worried about it.

---

40 Benjamin, B. & Werner R. (n.d.). *The Primacy of Human Touch*, HEALTH Newsletter. http://www.benbenjamin.com/articles.html

41 Greene, M. (2017, August 07). *Touch Isolation: How Homophobia Has Robbed All Men of Touch*. Retrieved from https://medium.com/@remakingmanhood/touch-isolation-how-homophobia-has-robbed-all-men-of-touch-239987952f16.

42 McKay, B & McKay K., *"Bosom Buddies: A Photo History of Male Affection,"* (http://artofmanliness.com).

A friend once told me that he has a rule of thumb when it comes to physical affection: *"Whatever is a legitimate way to love a small child, I will willingly step into. If young boys need it then why not grown men? How are young men going to get their needs met otherwise? By praying? By reading scripture? By going to church?"* Although these are positive activities, they certainly aren't going to fill the need for affection or heal attachment wounds. God wants us to meet our needs for affection and heal any wounds surrounding it.

Laura Brotherson, a marriage and family educator, believes that if we do not address unmet needs, including touch deprivation, sexual confusion or problems often escalate. She believes that these deficits make people more susceptible to problematic sexual behavior. An awareness of this need for physical affection, and efforts to give and receive it, can fill the deficit and reduce the problematic behavior. She also believes that people often confuse restless feelings for affection with other sensations like sexual desire or stomach hunger.[43]

It is important to understand that all humans are wired for physical affection. Some have never received it, and others were touched in abusive or manipulative ways. However, healthy affection enhances our attachment and provides much-needed physical contact and connection.

---

43 Brotherson, L. (n.d.). StrengtheningMarriage.com. Retrieved July 28, 2018, from https://www.strengtheningmarriage.com/

Chapter 14 Questions

1. Write about a time you were starved for touch.

_____

_____

_____

_____

_____

_____

_____

_____

_____

_____

2. What positive experiences have you had with touch and affection?

_____

_____

_____

_____

_____

_____

_____

_____

_____

3. What negative experiences have you had with touch and affection?

_____

_____

_____

_____

_____

_____

_____

_____

4. Can you think of mentors or buddies from whom you'd like to receive healthy affection? List them here.

_____

_____

_____

_____

_____

_____

_____

_____

_____

_____

5. What beliefs do you have about touch that make things more difficult? (For example: *"Men aren't supposed to touch each other,"* or *"Men shouldn't need affection – they should be tough.")*

_____

_____

_____

_____

_____

_____

_____

_____

_____

6. Can you think of an example of healthy touch from a story or movie you've seen? Please describe what you saw.

_____

_____

_____

_____

_____

_____

_____

7. Can you think of an example of healthy touch from a Biblical story? Please describe.

_____

_____

_____

_____

_____

_____

_____

8. ACTION ASSIGNMENT: During the week watch for examples of other boys and men showing healthy affection for one another. Write here what you observed.

_____

_____

_____

_____

_____

_____

_____

_____

_____

Chapter 15

Attachment Counterfeits
Porn & Experimentation

When a young man is already hungry for legitimate attachment, he will be particularly vulnerable to pornography and experimentation. Emotions are fueled by starved attachment needs, so thoughts and fantasies can intensify. Sexual behavior can provide a counterfeit attachment. In other words, it feels like you're connecting, but there's no lasting bond.

As emotional pressure grows, arousal patterns get reinforced through sexual activity. The emotions below the surface aren't easily recognized, and the arousal patterns become intertwined with attachment needs. For some boys, sexual behavior becomes compulsive under these conditions. Longing for connection with other boys, new sexual instincts are easily pulled toward legitimate longings.

Envy fed my thoughts during junior high and high school. I daydreamed about potential friendships and activity. I was jealous of the interaction I observed in various groups and was deeply envious of other boys' connections with one another. I fantasized about a group of buddies with whom I could spend time. These thoughts and daydreams were ongoing and became sexualized when I discovered masturbation.

Pornography is everywhere in American culture. Most sociologists conclude that the first onset of exposure is between eight and eleven years old. Kids don't necessarily go looking for it, but sometimes it pops up before they understand what is happening.

The pornography industry hunts for ways to lure teens and children through various marketing schemes. Kids are naturally curious, and pornography preys on natural curiosity. Pornography is easy to find and retains a long-term profit strategy: Expose them as children and they pay money as adults.

Some youth find that pornography and sexual activity helps them to escape discomfort. Loneliness, isolation, depression, anxiety, or stress can be relieved through sexual behavior, which becomes a way to cope because it replicates connection. But it's a counterfeit form of connection.

Pornography also deposits novel ideas in the mind that increase curiosity or confusion. Patrick Carnes stated that porn addicts become focused on new types of behavior as they are exposed to new practices that were never originally part of their experience.[44] In some cases, young men describe new sexual interest in different activity based on images or videos they saw in pornography. It can teach unrealistic and unhealthy messages about human sexuality. Carnes goes on to explain that cybersex has the capacity to distort the arousal template by tapping into unresolved issues; that the arousal template can become altered.[45] In other words, sexual attraction may shift due to exposure.

Sometimes young men will start experimenting with other boys. This is not uncommon, and you shouldn't shame yourself for natural curiosity. Boys get curious about each other's bodies. However, if you have attachment deficits or wounds, you might be experimenting in ways that reflect those deficits or wounds. In this case, you will be reinforcing arousal patterns that stem from those deficits and wounds.

If you have already struggled with pornography or experimentation, DO NOT shame yourself. It's common for young men to be curious as they discover their sexuality. Don't be embarrassed to reach out for support. You can learn to manage your feelings.

You could be more prone to this temptation if you have attachment deficits or wounds. Porn reinforces sexual images in your mind and strengthens the arousal pattern. The images will become stronger over time. The more you look, the more you may want to look. This makes healing attachment wounds more difficult and time-consuming.

If you've tried to stop some form of sexual behavior but couldn't, and the activity has become unmanageable, then you might be developing an addiction. Porn-addiction is complex and has been referred to as the drug of a new generation.[46] You may need professional help to overcome it. I realize you may sometimes feel helpless about the problem, but you can escape its grasp. You can develop healthy ways of coping and overcome this addiction. You will have more peace and happiness if you make the hard choice to ask for help. Seek adult mentors you can trust to support you. You are not alone with this struggle, so don't be ashamed.

---

44 Carnes, P., & Carnes, P. (2001). *Out of the shadows: Understanding sexual addiction.* Center City, MN: Hazelden Information & Edu, p.85.

45 Carnes, P., & Carnes, P. (2001). *Out of the shadows: Understanding sexual addiction.* Center City, MN: Hazelden Information & Edu, p 91.

46 Kastleman, M. B. (2001). *The drug of the new millennium: The science of how internet pornography radically alters the human brain and body.* Orem, UT: Granite Pub.

In addition to masturbation and pornography, it is possible for a boy to be the victim of sexual abuse or molestation. When abuse occurs in childhood, it awakens sexual feelings before the victim is ready and may cause them to move in unhealthy directions. For example, a boy who has been sexually abused might repeat sexual activity as a way of coping. This is called trauma-reenactment. If you've been abused, make sure and spend adequate time in the chapter about abuse.

It's also important for you to understand that one's sexual behavior is NOT necessarily about love. Sexuality is powerful and can be difficult to manage. There will be curiosity and excitement during adolescence, but these urges don't need to consume you. Sexual behavior can become addictive, so be cautious about the ways you experiment. As a young man you are wired for sexuality.[47]

---

47 Carnes, P. (2001). *Out of the shadows: Understanding sexual addiction.* Center City, MN: Hazelden, p.14.

Chapter 15 Questions

1. What feelings do you have when talking about sexual things?

☐ Embarrassed ☐ Scared ☐ Shy ☐ Funny

☐ Humiliated ☐ Excited ☐ Curious ☐ Guilty

☐ Anxious ☐ Ashamed ☐ Interested ☐ Nervous

☐ Vulnerable ☐ Bored ☐ Aroused ☐ Shame

☐ Other _____

☐ Other _____

2. Which of the feelings listed above are strongest? Please describe.

_____

_____

_____

_____

_____

_____

3. How old were you when you started puberty, and what were the first changes in your body that you noticed?

_____

_____

_____

4. Write about a time you felt confused or embarrassed about the changes in your body.

_____

_____

_____

_____

5. How old were you when you first had the "sex talk?" Who talked to you? Where were you? What was it like?

_____

_____

_____

_____

_____

_____

6. When do you remember feeling "confused" about sexual things? Please describe.

_____

_____

_____

_____

_____

7. What are your moral beliefs about sex? What is right and wrong?

_____

_____

_____

_____

_____

8. Make a complete list of all the sexual things you've ever done. Think back as early as you can remember. Share this list with your counselor.

_____

_____

_____

_____

_____

_____

_____

_____

9. Are you doing things that might be reinforcing the arousal pattern?

_____

_____

_____

_____

_____

_____

_____

10. Discuss each of the following questions with a trusted male mentor. Some of the questions may cause you to think of other questions. Remember that curiosity isn't bad, so don't be afraid to talk about it. Be brave and ask any additional questions that arise during the discussion.

- Were you embarrassed to talk about puberty and sex when you were a teenager?

- How did you first learn about sex?

- How did you learn about puberty and the changes to your body?

- What were the first body changes you noticed?

- How old are most boys and girls when they start puberty?

- Did you start changing before or after your friends?

- How often are wet dreams supposed to happen?

- Is it normal to have erections when you DON'T feel sexual?

- When are you supposed to start shaving?

- Do you remember having B.O. and using deodorant?

- Am I supposed to be thinking about sex all the time?

- Is it normal if I'm not obsessed with girls?

- Did you ever masturbate when you were a teenager?

- How do I know if my penis is a normal size or shape?

- As a teenager, did you ever have sexual thoughts just pop into your head?

- What was dating like for you as a teenager?

- What are your personal morals or beliefs about healthy sexual activity?

- Did you ever watch pornography?

11. What additional questions came from this discussion?

_____

_____

_____

_____

_____

_____

_____

_____

12. Now go back and circle the most embarrassing questions. Explain to your counselor and mentor why these were the most embarrassing.

_____

_____

_____

_____

_____

_____

_____

_____

11. What are the sexual behaviors you need to stop as a part of recovery?

_____

_____

_____

_____

_____

_____

_____

_____

_____

Chapter 16

Attachment Counterfeit
Sexual Addiction

As mentioned previously, when a young man is hungry for legitimate attachment, he will be particularly vulnerable to sexual exploration. Sexual urges are heightened by starved attachment needs so thoughts and fantasies can become obsessive. It's this obsessive nature that leads to addiction.

In her research on sexual addiction, Alexandra Katehakis noted how insecure attachments often drive sex addicts like a drug.[48] It's this obsessive quality that can sweep a young man into the depths of sexual addiction. Behaviors that are compulsive will generate an inability to control and interfere with one's life.[49] It becomes a drug to provide temporary relief from the attachment wounds and other distressing emotions. Even the anticipation of sexual activity can create a 'high' for the addict.[50]

Patrick Carnes said that for sex addicts, it's the "sex" that makes isolation tolerable.[51] Sexually addictive behavior provides a counterfeit source of attachment – it feels like you're connecting, but there's no intimate relationship or lasting bond. The relationship becomes about sex, not people.[52]

Emotional dynamics below the surface are inherently related to attachment needs and wounds. The deficits create an emotional vacuum and can become an emotional preoccupation. This pre-addictive emotional state can lead toward sexually addictive behavior.

Because there's no substantial bonding in sexually compulsive behavior, young men are often left with a sense of emptiness and loneliness when they act out. It's

48 Katehakis, A. (2016). *Sex addiction as affect dysregulation: A neurobiologically informed holistic treatment.* New York: W. W. Norton & company, p. 33.

49 Wilson, G. (2017). *Your brain on porn: Internet pornography and the emerging science of addiction.* Margate, Kent, United Kingdom: Commonwealth Publishing, p. 24.

50 Weiss, R., & Schneider, J. P. (2015). *Always turned on: Sex addiction in the digital age.* Carefree, AZ: Gentle Path Press, p. 34.

51 Carnes, P., & Carnes, P. (2001). *Out of the shadows: Understanding sexual addiction.* Center City, MN: Hazelden Information & Edu, p.16.

52 Carnes, P., & Carnes, P. (2001), *Out of the shadows: Understanding sexual addiction.* Center City, MN: Hazelden Information & Edu, p.16.

been noted by Patrick Carnes that sexual addiction is partially rooted in the fear of rejection.[53] This is why therapists often refer to addiction as a "disease of isolation."[54]

Masturbation is often the first sexually compulsive behavior for teenage boys. It becomes a habit they cannot stop. Some masturbation would be common, but when it grows into compulsive forms of escape, it becomes unhealthy. If a boy already daydreams about attachment with boys, his new sexual urges make it easy to masturbate to those emotional fantasies.

However, underneath the sexual behavior lies the unresolved emotional struggle. Rob Weiss commented that withdrawal symptoms for a sex addict often include things like depression, anxiety, low self-esteem, or trauma. This manifests itself in forms of loneliness, neediness, anger, fear, or unhappiness.[55] There will always be some underlying emotional issues at the root of addiction. This was certainly true for me.

I accidentally discovered masturbation during junior high. Although a bit frightening, it gave me an instant high. I turned to it whenever I felt lonely or depressed. My envy of boys at school got me thinking about them and my lack of friends made me jealous of their friendships. I was deeply envious of their connection with one another. I fantasized about a group of buddies with whom I could spend time. These thoughts and daydreams were ongoing and became sexualized. It became a compulsive habit which I couldn't stop. It also provided relief from the emotional distress I was experiencing.

Pornography is easy to find and often becomes the next step toward sexual addiction. Pornography becomes a drug and, according to Gary Wilson, the science proving this is overwhelming.[56] One researcher called internet pornography the "crack cocaine" of sexual addiction.[57] Most boys will be exposed to pornography between the ages of eight and eleven, but young men with sexualized attachments may turn to pornography as a way of diminishing the pain and loneliness of the attachment

---

53 Carnes, P., & Carnes, P. (2001), p.29.

54 Flores, P. J. (2012). *Addiction as an attachment disorder.* Lanham: Jason Aronson, p.148.

55 Weiss, R., & Schneider, J. P. (2015). *Always turned on: Sex addiction in the digital age.* Carefree, AZ: Gentle Path Press, p. 134.

56 Wilson, G. (2017). *Your brain on porn: Internet pornography and the emerging science of addiction.* Margate, Kent, United Kingdom: Commonwealth Publishing, p. 75.

57 Cooper, Delmonico, and Burg, "Cybersex Users, Abusers, and Compulsives: New Findings and Implications," *Sexual Addiction and Compulsivity: The Journal of Treatment and Prevention 7*, nos. 1-2 (2000), as cited by Carnes, P., & Carnes, P. (2001). *Out of the shadows: Understanding sexual addiction.* Center City, MN: Hazelden Information & Edu, p. 84.

wounds.[58] Gary Wilson stated that it's very common to feel anxious or depressed when isolated.[59] Like masturbation, pornography can provide a chemical high that helps a young man escape the realities of his painful existence.

Sexually addictive behavior provides an escape from emotional distress. Feelings of loneliness, depression, anxiety, or fear can be allayed through sexual behavior. Consequently, the behavior becomes a way to cope and becomes increasingly addictive over time. Rob Weiss said that most sex addicts use sexual activity as a way of escaping emotional discomfort. In the end however, this only magnifies any feelings of loneliness, fear, isolation, and unhappiness. He continues to say that the underlying issue relates to this longing for intimacy and attachment.[60] Addicts often regress as isolation increases, ultimately losing intimacy instead of creating or improving it.[61]

Sometimes early experimentation with other boys can lead to sexually compulsive behavior. This is not uncommon, and you shouldn't shame yourself for curiosity, but remember that your brain is trying to cope with all these new emotions inside. Early experimentation can escalate over time.

If you are feeling consumed by sexual urges and have started acting out compulsively, be honest about the possibility that you're addicted. Sexual addiction takes everything to a new level. You will need a professional counselor trained in sexual addiction to guide you toward recovery. Compulsive behavior only reinforces loneliness and often reenacts trauma and pain which has occurred. Your sexual behavior might provide temporary relief from your troubles, along with a 'high,' but doesn't provide the lasting peace you're looking for.

You will be prone to sexual addiction if you have attachment deficits, failures, or wounds. Addiction makes recovery more time-consuming because you'll now be working harder to eliminate sexually addictive behavior from your life. You will have an added aspect of recovery involving addiction, but you can overcome your compulsions.

If you are addicted and have not been able to stop, it does not mean you are

58 What's the Average Age of Someone's First Exposure to Porn? (2018, May 04). Retrieved July 24, 2018, from https://fightthenewdrug.org/real-average-age-of-first-exposure/

59 Wilson, G. (2017). *Your brain on porn: Internet pornography and the emerging science of addiction.* Margate, Kent, United Kingdom: Commonwealth Publishing, p. 109.

60 Weiss, R. (2015). *Sex addiction 101: A basic guide to healing from sex, porn, and love addiction.* Deerfield Beach, FL: Health Communications, p.141.

61 Carnes, P., & Carnes, P. (2001). *Out of the shadows: Understanding sexual addiction.* Center City, MN: Hazelden Information & Edu, p.85.

a pervert. Sexual addiction is complex. It is the drug of a new generation.[62] You will need professional help and education to conquer it. But, as impossible as it seems, you *can* escape its grasp. You can develop healthy ways to manage your sexual urges. You will have more peace and happiness if you make the hard choice to get help. Find adult mentors and sponsors that can love you while you seek professional help. You are not the only one with this struggle, so don't be ashamed.

Sex addicts will often struggle with deep negative core beliefs about themselves that prevents them from seeking help and support.[63] If you can identify with any of the four statements below, then your own core beliefs will be contributing to sexual addiction:

1. I am a bad and unworthy person.

2. No one could ever love me the way I am.

3. I cannot trust or depend on others to meet my needs.

4. Life without sex seems impossible.

As we discussed previously, sexual abuse magnifies pre-addiction dynamics. Sexual abuse awakens sexual feelings and may cause some boys to move into sexual compulsions. For example, some boys might repeat the sexual behavior that happened during the abuse as a way of coping. Called trauma reenactment, this is a common pre-addiction dynamic.[64]

Remember that sexual addiction is NOT about love, but rather an attempt by the brain to regulate emotions and attachment wounds. Sexual behavior can become addictive, so be cautious and don't be afraid to seek professional help.[65]

Sharing your story is a powerful step in recovery. Forest Benedict said that "Letting safe people see into the dark places within can be an incredibly frightening yet healing experience."[66] There are support programs available. Sex Addicts Anonymous says in their green book that, "We pick someone we trust to hear our inventory… and

---

62 How Porn Affects the Brain Like a Drug. (2018, June 26). Retrieved from https://fightthenewdrug.org/how-porn-affects-the-brain-like-a-drug/.

63 Carnes, P. (1994). *Contrary to love: Helping the sexual addict.* Center City, MN: Hazelden Foundation, p 87.

64 Van, B. A. (1989, June). The compulsion to repeat the trauma. Re-enactment, revictimization, and masochism. Retrieved from https://www.ncbi.nlm.nih.gov/pubmed/2664732.

65 Carnes, P. (2001). *Out of the shadows: Understanding sexual addiction.* Center City, MN: Hazelden, p.14.

66 Benedict, F. (2017). *Life After Lust - Stories & Strategies for Sex & Pornography Addiction Recovery.* Visionary Books, p. 117.

who already knows and accepts us unconditionally."[67] It's often a fear of being judged that builds a wall around us, preventing us from sharing. There can be an intense fear of exposure that others might see our badness and reject us.[68] Remember that your recovery and spiritual growth depend on recognizing that you need help and cannot do it alone.[69] We are wired for attachment and community.

Sometimes reaching out to someone you trust actually helps to decrease the shame you feel, which then helps you to stop. An interesting study by Joshua Grubbs considered that personal values can make it feel like you're addicted to pornography. In other words, the more shameful and worried you feel, the more you might perceive you are addicted to it.[70] He did another study a few years later and found the same thing: "...moral disapproval and moral incongruence (i.e., feeling as if one's behaviors and one's values about those behaviors are misaligned) might specifically contribute to self-perceived problems around pornography use."[71] Considering this, you might want to talk to someone about how your personal values are contributing to your anxiety with pornography.

Nonetheless, pornography can be very addictive. Some interesting medical research was done by Dr. Voon from Cambridge University. She performed MRI scans for people who struggle with compulsive sexual behavior.[72] The results clearly show areas of the brain which get rewired by compulsive sexual behavior. It changes our impulse-control, emotional capacity, and social interaction.[73] What does that mean? It means you'll slowly become more impulsive and have increased difficulty with emotion and social interaction. Dr. Don Hilton suggests that we are wired for sexual intimacy with a person, not a computer monitor. He says that young men who are accustomed to having sex with a computer screen will find it unlikely that a woman

67 *Sex Addicts Anonymous.* (2017). Houston, TX: International Service Organization SAA, p. 38.

68 Carnes, P. (1994). *Contrary to love: Helping the sexual addict.* Center City, MN: Hazelden Foundation, p. 119.

69 Ryan, T. C. (2012). *Ashamed No More: A Pastor's Journey Through Sex Addiction.* InterVarsity Press, p. 102.

70 Grubbs, J. B., Carlisle, R., Hook, J., Pargament, K., & Exline, J. J. (2015, January). *Transgression as addiction: religiosity and moral disapproval as predictors of perceived addiction to pornography.* Archives of sexual behavior. https://pubmed.ncbi.nlm.nih.gov/24519108/.

71 Grubbs, J., & Perry, S. (2018). Moral Incongruence and Pornography Use: A Critical Review and Integration. *The Journal of Sex Research,* 1–34. https://doi.org/10.1080/00224499.2018.1427204

72 Voon, V., Mole, T. B., Banca, P., Porter, L., Morris, L., Mitchell, S., . . . Irvine, M. (2014, July 11). Neural correlates of sexual cue reactivity in individuals with and without compulsive sexual behaviours. Retrieved from https://www.ncbi.nlm.nih.gov/pmc/articles/PMC4094516/

73 Wilson, G. (2017). *Your brain on porn: Internet pornography and the emerging science of addiction.* Margate, Kent, United Kingdom: Commonwealth Publishing, p. 92.

will fit the bill.[74] It changes how your brain functions. It will have an impact on your emotions and social interaction. Some young men will report that they start to have problems with normal arousal. They notice they don't get erections in the same way after extensive pornography use. Some will say that it's even becoming difficult to feel aroused by a regular girl; almost like they're experiencing ED (erectile dysfunction). Some research indicates this is untrue, but it's commonly reported in recovery groups.[75]

On a final note, remember that you aren't necessarily addicted just because you keep doing it. Most young men find pornography extremely enticing but are not addicted to it.[76] Ongoing pornography or sexual behavior can reinforce the patterns you've created, but just because you keep acting out doesn't mean you're addicted. Whether you think you're addicted or not, you'll want to consider what things need to change for good healing and recovery.

74 VIDEO: Neurosurgeon Dr. Donald Hilton Reveals Shocking Scientific Truths About Porn. (n.d.). Retrieved July 28, 2018, from https://fightthenewdrug.org/media/neurosurgeon-donald-hilton-jr-truths-about-porn-harms-brain.

75 Grubbs, J., & Gola, M. (2019). Is Pornography Use Related to Erectile Functioning? Results From Cross-Sectional and Latent Growth Curve Analyses. *The Journal of Sexual Medicine*, 16(1), 111–125. https://doi.org/https://doi.org/10.1016/j.jsxm.2018.11.004

76 othe, B., Toth-Kieraly, I., Potenza, M., Gabor, O., & Demetrovics, Z. (2020). High-Frequency Pornography Use May Not Always Be Problematic. *The Journal of Sexual Medicine*, 1–20. https://doi.org/10.1016/j.jsxm.2020.01.007

Chapter 16 Questions

1. What feelings do you have when talking about sexual addiction?

❑ Embarrassed   ❑ Scared   ❑ Shy   ❑ Funny

❑ Humiliated   ❑ Excited   ❑ Curious   ❑ Guilty

❑ Anxious   ❑ Ashamed   ❑ Interested   ❑ Nervous

❑ Vulnerable   ❑ Bored   ❑ Aroused   ❑ Shame

❑ Other _____

❑ Other _____

2. Take the following quiz to see about the possibility of sexual addiction. If you can answer most of the questions as YES, then consult with a professional counselor about possible sex addiction:

YES/NO   Have you worried something might be wrong with you?

YES/NO   Have you felt depressed about your behavior?

YES/NO   Have you felt anxiety or panic about your behavior?

YES/NO   Have you ever felt as though you couldn't stop?

YES/NO   Have you continued the behavior when it was against your core beliefs or values?

YES/NO   Have you tried to stop but always failed?

YES/NO   Have you felt the urges were stronger than you?

YES/NO   Do your behaviors ever get in the way of other things?

YES/NO   Is it almost all you think about?

YES/NO   Does the behavior help you to relax or feel better?

YES/NO   Does the behavior help you escape stress or life?

YES/NO   Does the behavior remind you of previous abuse?

YES/NO   Do you spend time trying to hide your behavior?

3. Have you been involved in sexting behavior including pics of yourself? Describe below and discuss with your therapist.

_____

_____

_____

4. Has anyone been upset about your sexual activities?
Describe below and discuss with your therapist.

_____

_____

_____

_____

5. Have you ever engaged in sexually "risky" behaviors?
Describe below and discuss with your therapist.

_____

_____

_____

_____

6. Have you ever traded sexual behavior for money or gifts?
Describe below and discuss with your therapist.

_____

_____

_____

_____

7. How long do you spend on pornography each day?
Describe below and discuss with your therapist.

_____

_____

_____

_____

_____

8. What types of images or videos do you watch on pornography?
Describe below and discuss with your therapist.

_____

_____

_____

_____

9. How do you spend time trying to hide your sexual behavior?
Describe below and discuss with your therapist.

_____

_____

_____

_____

10. Is there any aspect of your sexual behavior that you believe might be abnormal?
Describe below and discuss with your therapist.

_____

_____

_____

_____

11. Have you been tempted to be sexual with older adults?
Describe below and discuss with your therapist.

_____

_____

_____

_____

_____

12. Is there anything about your sexual behavior that might be "unsafe?" Describe below and discuss with your therapist.

_____

_____

_____

_____

13. What sexual behaviors do you need to stop as a part of addiction recovery? These would be your "bottom lines." List them below and discuss with your therapist.

_____

_____

_____

_____

_____

14. There are various programs and professional counselors that can help you with sexual addiction. Do a Google search and list the possible resources in your area. List them below and discuss with your therapist.

_____

_____

_____

_____

_____

_____

_____

Chapter 17

Attachment Confusion
Sexual Abuse

If you were sexually abused, someone violated your boundaries. They ignored your needs and may have caused you to feel diminished. Your body was used by someone else for their own manipulation or pleasure. It generally creates emotional or physical pain, confusing sexual feelings, discomfort with one's own body, and general insecurity about yourself.[77]

If you have been sexually abused, then you're not alone. Some boys with sexualized attachments were abused. One of the most common symptoms of sexual abuse is confusion. Abused kids often worry they might be abnormal or homosexual.[78] The abuse itself can be at the root of your confusion as noted by various therapists.[79] For some boys, the abuse is the worst thing that has ever happened. It's unfair. Did something happen to you? Has someone older than you taken advantage of you in ways you didn't understand?

Even teenagers get sexually abused by other young men or adults. When anyone is sexually abused, it causes emotional injury. It generates wounding around attachment needs. In some ways, it's like being physically injured. If you were to break your leg while playing in the yard with friends, you'd need help from others. Although it would be an unfair situation, you'd need someone to pick you up, set the broken bones, apply the cast, support you when you cannot walk, and provide comfort when you're in pain.

While emotional injury is not always obvious, avoiding help can cause these injuries to fester. It leaves invisible scars that cannot be seen, but which are felt inside. NOT dealing with the abuse leaves you with injuries to thoughts and feelings. However, you can heal and find peace from the pain and confusion the abuse has created. It takes time and requires help from others. It takes patience and hard work,

---

77 Timms, R. J., & Connors, P. (1999). *Embodying healing: Integrating bodywork and psychotherapy in recovery from childhood sexual abuse.* Brandon, VT: Safer Society Press, p. 9.

78 Wright, L. B., & Loiselle, M. B. (1997). *Back on track: Boys dealing with sexual abuse.* Brandon: Safer Society Press, p.78-79.

79 Kort, J., & Morgan, A. P. (2014). *Is my husband gay, straight, or bi?: A guide for women concerned about their men.* Lanham: Rowman & Littlefield, p. xv.

but you can heal.

What is abuse? If you were tricked, misled, deceived, forced, bribed, or threatened into sexual behavior by anyone who had more power than you, then it's abuse. ANY sexual contact with a child by someone older than the child, is considered abuse. Even if the child seemed willing – it's still abuse. Children cannot give true consent for such behavior because they aren't mature or experienced. The interaction is more than they are equipped to handle. Similarly, if someone touched you sexually without your permission or knowledge, that is abuse. Some boys get taken advantage of while they are sleeping or grabbed before they have time to react. These are equally abusive situations.

One of the biggest problems for boys who are sexually abused is that they often don't talk about it. If you've been sexually abused, you might not have the right words to express what happened to you or how you feel about it. That's okay. Don't worry about saying the right things. When you're ready, the words will come. You'll just need to talk. To heal emotional wounds, it's important to talk.

Some boys don't tell anyone about the abuse because they are afraid of getting in trouble. Perhaps it happened when they were away from home, or maybe they were doing something they weren't supposed to do, or perhaps went somewhere they weren't supposed to be. Other boys don't tell because they think they should handle it on their own. They want to be tough. In some instances, boys are angry with themselves because they didn't stop what was happening. In other cases, they are afraid people won't believe it happened. Even worse, some boys are afraid the person who abused them will harm them in some way. Abusive people will sometimes be threatening. Sexual abuse is hard to stop by yourself. You need support from safe adults.

Another problem is when the abuse doesn't feel like abuse. For example, maybe it just felt like goofing off or playing around. The feelings it aroused may have been pleasurable. Let's face it, a boy's private parts are sensitive and playing with them can be arousing. To further confuse the situation, an abuser may have been someone the victim admired or trusted.[80] I've heard boys say, *"I don't feel abused. I really liked the guy."* Even when abuse doesn't feel like abuse, it's still damaging and confusing. It messes with your legitimate needs for attachment, affection, and affirmation.

---

80 Wright, L. B., & Loiselle, M. B. (1997). *Back on track: Boys dealing with sexual abuse.* Brandon: Safer Society Press, P. 37.

HEALING & RECOVERY

Confusion

A young boy's natural attachment needs are wounded by abuse. What are these needs? They could include need for mentoring, need for physical affection, and need for acceptance or affirmation. With abuse, someone older is hijacking natural needs and sexualizing them.

For example, if you were already starved for a mentor, it would make it hard for you to resist sexual advances by an older boy or adult that you admired. He may have been feeding your need for approval, bonding, and validation. If he reached out to spend time with you, and then sexualized the time you spent together, your need to be mentored is confused with sexual feelings. Your natural attachment drive has been hijacked.

The need for physical affection is no less important. As I explained in a previous chapter, we all need touch. If you were naturally seeking affection in healthy ways, and someone started sexualizing the touch, your natural need for affection becomes confused. Your brain starts to associate touch and affection with sexuality. After a while, physical affection and touch could start to feel sexual. Your natural need for affection gets hijacked.

Boys want to feel accepted. If an older male befriends a younger boy, then sexualizes their interaction as part of the inclusion, the younger boy's natural need for acceptance becomes confused. Sexual activity becomes a way of receiving acceptance. The boy's brain interprets sexual activity as a form of acceptance. His natural attachment need for acceptance and connection gets hijacked.

It is natural for a boy to need mentoring, affection, and acceptance. But those needs should never be met in sexual ways. Your natural feelings get thrown off course. It could make the abuse feel okay because "I wanted it." You wanted mentoring, affection, acceptance, approval, or friendship – not sex.

Natural Design

Your genitals are naturally designed to be sensitive and ticklish. That's not bad and it's not wrong. You don't have to feel guilt or shame about it. Your genitals can elicit exciting and powerful feelings. However, someone may have tricked or forced you to awaken these feelings too soon. You may have been too young to understand them. This was not your fault.

Every young man has traits wired into him that will help him grow into manhood. Some of these qualities include curiosity, adventure, and play. When men are naturally curious, adventurous, and playful, they excel at their careers and professions. They become men who can provide for a family. However, these same qualities make boys targets of abuse. Natural curiosity can lead boys toward sexual exploration. The desire for play can lead a boy toward games that lead to sexual activity. The need for adventure could also drive a boy toward *"I dare you"* type activities.

You don't need to feel bad about having these traits. Embrace them. Used in a healthy way they are strengths and will lead you toward healthy masculinity. However, it is abusive when others take advantage of these qualities to lure you into sexual activity.

The Healing Process

You will start the process of emotional healing by recognizing that the sexual abuse was NOT YOUR FAULT. If abuse has made you feel bad about yourself, that's a problem. Remember it was not your fault. Even if you believe that you caused it, or that you wanted to do it, chances are you were too young to know better. Yes… even as a teenager. When abuse happens, boys and teens don't have the ability to completely understand what is happening.

A common symptom of abuse is Toxic Shame. It's okay to feel remorse, but you don't have to feel bad about yourself. Toxic shame is different from guilt or remorse. It's toxic because we get the message that we're worthless.[81] It robs you of self-esteem and confidence and makes you feel like a loser. It's okay to acknowledge that something happened, but it's wrong to think it defines who you are. Look at the chart below.

OKAY (Guilt)	WRONG (Toxic Shame)
"It was bad…"	"I am bad."
"It was a mistake…"	"I am a mistake…"
"It was wrong…"	"Something is wrong with me…"

Toxic shame is like emotional cancer. You've got to stop it from killing you inside. Nothing is wrong with YOU! You didn't know. You didn't understand. The worst thing you can do is harbor toxic shame about yourself. A prominent therapist named Rob Weiss often works with victims of abuse and said that childhood abuse

---

81 Ryan, T. C. (2012). *Ashamed No More: A Pastors Journey Through Sex Addiction*. InterVarsity Press, p. 68.

leaves victims feeling both confusion and shame.[82]

You might have noticed the more alone you remain with your secret, the more shame grows. Shame thrives in isolation. You need to come out of the dark and get support. Now is the time to tell someone. Let a light shine into the dark corner of your life. I realize this is scary if you've been hiding it.

When you finally open up, people won't always know how to respond correctly. Rather than patiently listening to what you are reporting, they may experience their own emotions about the abuse. Sometimes they say things that make it worse; they may ask thoughtless questions. If they do, these questions reflect their own insecurities. Don't take on the toxic shame. Here are some ridiculous questions:

- *"Why did you let this happen?"*

- *"Why didn't you scream or call out?"*

- *"Why didn't you tell me sooner?"*

- *"Why didn't you run away?"*

Check out some additional BAD and UNHEALTHY responses:

- **Shocked** – Some people react in a "shocked" way and make you feel worse. They act like being sexually abused is the worst possible thing to ever happen.

- **Scared** – Some people become overly worried or scared and can make you more worried or scared.

- **Angry** – Some people act mad when they find out a boy was abused. They might yell or scream. This response is hard.

- **Silent** – Some people just stay quiet because they don't know what to say. They don't know how to act and they become confused.

- **Sad** – Adults may feel extra sad and start shutting down. They might be overwhelmed with grief or get depressed.

- **Blame** – Some people may be shocked and want to assign blame for the abuse. They might say something like, "Why did you let him do that to you?" Others may even blame themselves, "I should have done more to protect you… I'm a terrible parent."

---

82 Weiss, R. (2015). *Sex addiction 101: A basic guide to healing from sex, porn, and love addiction.* Deerfield Beach, FL: Health Communications, p.66.

Don't be tricked by any of these negative responses from anyone. These are unhealthy responses by people who don't know what to do. Their bad response is not about you. They don't know what to do and they're doing the wrong thing. These responses can send you into toxic shame, so be cautious. It's the toxic shame that will propel you further into confusion. Sexual activity might then become a way to self-soothe, which tends to exacerbate shame and emotional discomfort.[83]

The following would be a list of healthy responses. These are the types of responses you would get from people who can really support you in recovery. They help to keep you away from toxic shame and feel good about yourself despite the abuse. Check these out.

Healthy Responses

- *"I love you and I'm here to help you through this crisis."*

- *"You are not alone. This has happened to other kids too."*

- *"What happened to you was not your fault. The only person who did wrong is the abuser."*

- *"We need to stop the other person from ever doing this to you, or to anyone else, ever again."*

- *"I want to protect you from this other person."*

- *"You have a lot of courage to tell me about this. I'm proud of you. You are really strong."*

- *"This really sucks that it happened, but you can get through this."*

- *"I want to be here for you."*

- *"I want to help you get through this. Let's work together on it."*

- *"Let's find a good counselor and a support group to help you heal."*

- *"I'm so sorry. Can I give you a hug?"*

- *"I'm so glad you told me! That took some courage."*

- *"I'm very proud of you for telling me. Let's fix this together."*

---

83 Weiss, R. (2015). *Sex addiction 101: A basic guide to healing from sex, porn, and love addiction.* Deerfield Beach, FL: Health Communications, p. 66.

One of the best things you can do for healing is to find a trusted adult and tell them what happened. One therapist noted that nothing reduces shame better than coming out of secrecy, sharing your story, and hearing others share similar stories.[84] Select someone who knows how to listen. If they can't listen, look for another person. Don't stop until you find someone you can trust to tell what happened. If you share what happened, you'll begin the healing process. It might be scary but coming out of isolation will help reduce shame. Try not to be discouraged if someone responds badly. Find someone else who CAN respond in a healthy manner.

A good counselor or mentor can help you and your family deal with trauma. They can assist you and your family to have open dialogue about emotion and rebuild your confidence. They can help you change self-destructive thoughts or behaviors caused by the abuse. They can give support and assurance to you and family members that you are not to blame for the abuser's behavior. They can help you feel normal again. Finally, they can teach skills necessary to take control of your body and prevent abuse in the future.

---

84 Katehakis, A. (2016). *Sex addiction as affect dysregulation: A neurobiologically informed holistic treatment.* New York: W. W. Norton & company, p. 225.

Chapter 17 Questions

1. Who took advantage of you sexually?

❑ Neighbor   ❑ Uncle   ❑ Stranger   ❑Camp counselor

❑ Father   ❑ Brother   ❑ Babysitter   ❑ Family friend

❑ Teacher   ❑ Cousin   ❑ Clergy   ❑ Stepdad

❑ Mother   ❑ Friend   ❑ Stepmom   ❑ Friend's parent

❑ Coach   ❑ Teenager   ❑ Other _____

2. Mark any of the following NORMAL needs that made you more vulnerable to the abuse.

❑ Need for mentor   ❑ Need for attention

❑ Need for acceptance   ❑ I wanted to be included

❑ I was looking for adventure   ❑ I was curious

❑ I was just being playful   ❑ Other _____

3. What happened felt abusive in the following ways:

❑ I was forced   ❑ I tried to stop it but couldn't

❑ It hurt me   ❑ It was scary and frightening

❑ I was raped   ❑ I couldn't stop it

❑ He manipulated me   ❑ I didn't know what was going on

❑ I was tricked   ❑ He took advantage of my size

❑ I didn't realize   ❑ It happened so fast that I couldn't respond

❑ Other _____   ❑ Other _____

4. I told someone and they had the following negative response:

❑ Shocked   ❑ Scared or worried

❑ Angry or mad   ❑ Silent

❑ Sadness   ❑ Blame

❑ Other _____

5. If someone had a negative response, write the story of what happened. Did you feel shame about their response?

_____

_____

_____

_____

_____

_____

_____

_____

_____

6. I never told anyone because…

❑ I didn't want to get in trouble.

❑ I was someplace I wasn't supposed to be.

❑ I should have stopped it.

❑ I felt like I could handle it alone.

❑ I didn't have anyone to tell.

❑ I wasn't sure what to say.

❑ It was too embarrassing.

❑ I didn't want to look like a wimp.

❑ No one would believe me.

❑ I was afraid what others would think.

❑ I didn't want anyone mad at me.

❑ I wasn't sure what to say.

❑ It felt like it was my fault.

❑ I felt guilty.

❑ I was afraid the abuser would hurt me.

❑ I was afraid no one would believe me.

7. List any adults you could possibly talk with about what happened.

_____

_____

_____

_____

8. When youth are abused, the perpetrator usually takes advantage of your natural needs for affection, approval, or affirmation. Before the abuse, how did these healthy needs show up? (For example, *"When I was little, I used to love it when my older brother would wrestle with me, or my dad would kiss me on the forehead..."*)

Affection:

_____

_____

_____

_____

_____

_____

_____

Approval:

_____

_____

_____

_____

_____

_____

Affirmation:

_____

_____

_____

_____

_____

9. Write the story of what happened to you. It doesn't matter whether it felt abusive or not, just get all the details down on paper. Discuss this both with a trusted mentor and your counselor.

_____

_____

_____

_____

_____

_____

Chapter 18

Attachment Influences
Genetic Dispositions

Genetic dispositions are qualities that each person has from birth. These traits are wired into you. Every boy has dispositions that make him unique from others, and we should celebrate the diversity. Additionally, attachment issues will both influence, and be influenced by, these dispositions. In other words, your bonding experiences will influence how your genetics express themselves. Likewise, your tendency to bond and connect will be influenced by your genetics.

In his book about addiction and attachment, P. Flores noted that attachment can alter gene expression.[85] This new area of research is called epigenetics and essentially looks at the way our environment alters or overrides the expression of genetic disposition.[86]

Here's an illustration: A young man is tall, has good eyesight, is coordinated, and strong. Does this imply he will automatically be a basketball player? Obviously not. It means he has a genetic *disposition* for basketball. He might be naturally gifted for athletics, but he must practice every day, shoot hoops, dribble the ball, scrimmage with friends, and get some coaching. Under the proper conditions, he becomes an excellent basketball player.

The opposite is also true. If he never touches a ball, never plays a game, never shoots hoops, or dribbles the ball, he will never rise to any skill with basketball. Although the genetic disposition is there, without proper training and effort, he will never be skilled at the game. It seems obvious to conclude that a person can have genetic dispositions that are awakened only when influenced by behavior and environment. This is the essence of epigenetic theory.[87]

In 1991, psychologists studied identical twins to look at genetics and sexuality.

---

85 Flores, P. J. (2012). Addiction as an attachment disorder. Lanham: Jason Aronson, p.161.

86 Weiss, R. (2015). *Sex addiction 101: A basic guide to healing from sex, porn, and love addiction.* Deerfield Beach, FL: Health Communications, p.60.

87 Weiss, R. (2015). *Sex addiction 101: A basic guide to healing from sex, porn, and love addiction.* Deerfield Beach, FL: Health Communications, p.60.

This was a great study because identical twins have identical DNA. If genetic factors determine sexual orientation, then both twins should have the same orientation. However, when tabulating sexual orientation, both twins experienced homosexual feelings only 52% of the time.[88] This important study revealed that genetics are only one factor in sexuality, and that attraction seems to be the product of a complex interaction between genetic disposition and environmental influence during childhood and adolescence.[89]

In considering genetic influences, you'll need to determine what dispositions are uniquely your own. These are traits you are born with that might contribute to your patterns. For example, a child may be born with an emotional or sensitive nature and is easily offended or hurt. When feelings are hurt, he may have a stronger tendency to pull away or detach. His sensitive disposition causes him to withdraw from bonding opportunities. In other words, his disposition makes him more vulnerable to attachment deficits. It's impossible to produce a comprehensive list of dispositions because the possibilities are endless, but some common examples might include being shy, fearful, anxious, stubborn, thin-skinned, creative, uncoordinated, introverted, depressed, withdrawn, timid, small, or sensitive.

My mother told me I was hyper-sensitive and stubborn. As you think back over my story, hopefully you can pick out some of my dispositions that contributed to my patterns. Take a minute to identify your own genetic dispositions and focus on how they influence your attachments.

Keep in mind that other young men who have similar dispositions often respond in different ways. Their reactions might have been different than your own. Their dispositions may not have influenced their arousal pattern in the same way, so don't shame or compare yourself. Don't waste emotional energy on regrets. You did the best you could with what you understood. Choose to move forward.

---

88 Bailey, J. M., & Pillard, R. C. (1991). *A Genetic Study of Male Sexual Orientation.* Archives of General Psychiatry,48(12), 1089. doi:10.1001/archpsyc.1991.01810360053008.

89 Kirk, M., & Madsen, H. (1990). *After the ball: How America will conquer its fear and hatred of gays in the 90s.* New York: Plume, p.184.

Chapter 18 Questions

1. Mark any of the dispositions below that describe you:

☐ Sensitive   ☐ Emotional   ☐ Tender   ☐ Stubborn

☐ Timid   ☐ Hard-headed   ☐ Fearful   ☐ Anxious

☐ Shy   ☐ Analytical   ☐ Creative   ☐ Non-athletic

☐ Musical   ☐ Thin-skinned   ☐ Artistic   ☐ Needy

☐ Other _____   ☐ Other _____

☐ Other _____   ☐ Other _____

2. Explain how dispositions marked above come out in your personality?

_____

_____

_____

_____

_____

_____

3. Explain how these dispositions contribute to your patterns?

_____

_____

_____

_____

_____

_____

_____

_____

4. Write about an incident when you remember a disposition made it harder to connect with mentors. (For example, *"I was so sensitive… my coach's reaction seemed harsh so I…"*).

_____

_____

_____

_____

_____

_____

_____

5. Tell about a time you remember that a disposition made it harder to connect with other boys. (For example, *"I was shy, so I never hung out with the other guys…"*).

_____

_____

_____

_____

_____

_____

_____

_____

6. Tell about a time you remember that a disposition made it harder to feel masculine and confident. (For example, *"I was small and skinny... so I avoided tryouts for the team..."*).

_____

_____

_____

_____

_____

_____

_____

_____

7. Tell about a time you remember that a disposition made it easier or harder to connect with girls. (For example, *"I liked talking... the girls wanted to talk..."*).

_____

_____

_____

_____

_____

_____

_____

_____

8. Write down your understanding of how your own unique genetic dispositions contributed to your patterns.

_____

_____

_____

_____

_____

_____

_____

_____

_____

_____

_____

_____

Chapter 19

Adjusting Your Filter

If you have sexualized attachments, then you've probably developed a filter in your mind through which you view yourself and the world. This filter might cause you to see common experiences as abnormal. You might give yourself labels which are incorrect. Perhaps early in life you perceived yourself as different, when in truth other boys were sharing similar fears and apprehensions. It's unfortunate when boys misunderstand common experiences, filter them into an abnormal category, and label themselves as something different.

Viewing yourself as broken or abnormal is unhealthy. It leaves you feeling distant from others, not connected. Healing and recovery must involve the reversal of any alienation.[90] It reflects a need to adjust your filter about how you perceive yourself with others in the world. Perceptions of yourself can strengthen incorrect labels. You are normal if you can relate to any of the following examples. These experiences might have been confusing, but they are common.

───────────────────────────────

CONFUSION: *"I wanted to be with boys more than girls."*

REALITY: It's normal for boys to desire the company of other boys. It's part of the normal drive for attachment and connection. Boys like to be with other boys. Oftentimes they become angry when girls interfere in buddy relationships. Some examples: a group of younger boys create a "boys-only" club and become frustrated when girls try to join; a school dance where most boys stand together and encourage each other; buddies who become jealous when one leaves the group to spend time with a girlfriend.

───────────────────────────────

90 Carnes, P., & Carnes, P. (2001). *Out of the shadows: Understanding sexual addiction.* Center City, MN: Hazelden Information & Edu, p.31.

CONFUSION: *"I was curious about other boys' bodies and how they compared to mine."*

REALITY: At a very early age children become curious about their own body and how it compares to others. During puberty most boys have a renewed curiosity as their body experiences new physical changes. Teens are often intrigued by how the changes compare to others their own age. Muscle growth, body hair, and other changes emerge as boys mature. Sometimes in the locker room boys will look at each other to see or compare. They soon discover that there are a variety of differences between individual body types. Curiosity is normal.

~~~~~~

CONFUSION: *"I felt drawn toward men and boys who were attractive, athletic and popular."*

REALITY: Most people are drawn to others who are attractive in appearance or personality. Most men and boys like to be with others who are good-looking, successful, or popular. We all like to associate with people who we admire. We admire those with qualities we would like to possess. This appeal is a normal tendency, but boys hungry for connection will find this tendency to be magnified.

~~~~~~

CONFUSION: *"I was molested by someone… but I liked the attention – it felt good."*

REALITY: Abuse often happens with someone we admire or want to spend time with. We look at them as role models. We trust them and want to be close to them. It's confusing when they take advantage of this vulnerability. We want to be close to this person. Because our genitals are sensitive, they are easily stimulated. We are born this way. Whether a woman or a man touched you inappropriately, it could have produced pleasurable sensations, which means that everything is working correctly. Physical stimulation of your genitals causes more blood flow to the penis and an erection. The genital tissue swells because of the increased blood flow. A physical stimulus produces a physical response. This response can be pleasurable regardless of what causes it.

~~~~~~

CONFUSION: *"I got aroused when I was with the other boys."*

REALITY: Boys can become aroused in ways that are not directly sexual. An erection isn't always about attraction. Sometimes heightened emotions like fear or anxiety can cause an erection. For example, a boy might have an erection when he is called to speak in front of the class. The anxiety of the situation might cause the erection. Boys sometimes have spontaneous erections at unexpected moments without any reason. It can also happen when private parts rub against clothing, towels, etc., and a pleasurable sensation occurs. Puberty is a time of quick arousal, so simply being nude can trigger excitement (which can cause an awkward moment at the gym). Just because a boy has an erection, doesn't always mean it's sexual.

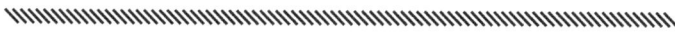

CONFUSION: *"I can't figure out who I am because of my attractions."*

REALITY: During adolescence, a young man can feel confused about his sexuality. Arousal patterns can fluctuate during this time depending upon life experiences and your emotional state. Sometimes traumatic events like rape or abuse can cause changes in sexual arousal. Young men should not define themselves by attraction or sexuality. Seek the guidance of loving mentors to help you in the process of discovery.

CONFUSION: *"I hate athletics and love music, art, and dance. Normal men love sports and don't enjoy those things."*

REALITY: In a culture obsessed with sports figures and athletic heroes, it's easy to understand how a young man who hasn't learned to play sports, or perhaps is uncoordinated, may feel out of place. Men and boys often don't participate in sports because they prefer other activities. Men who are more creative often prefer music and art. Even within athletics all men drift toward specific sports they prefer. Everyone's physical make-up is unique, so men drift toward activity that matches their body-type. For example, men with a larger frame might tend to prefer football, while thin or tall men may prefer basketball. Larger men could feel inadequate about basketball because it doesn't come as naturally. There is an endless variety of sports because there are so many different body types. It doesn't mean you're abnormal because you don't like sports. Additionally, some men weren't exposed to certain activities growing up and simply don't have familiarity with sports. This inhibits their enjoyment and participation.

CONFUSION: *"I'm not obsessed with girls, nor do I have a strong romantic interest in them."*

REALITY: Young boys are typically more interested in camaraderie with one another than they are with girls. Typical curiosity about the opposite sex is developed later, as boys begin to imagine themselves within romantic partnerships. They discuss this curiosity with male peers to the extent they feel safe and connected. These discussions reinforce male-bonding and give a young man courage to explore. Later, this curiosity blossoms into romantic attraction. Boys might try to kiss or hold hands with a girl. Romantic feelings are developed as he matures. However, it's also important to note that some boys never feel obsessed with girls. It can be normal to be interested without being obsessed.

\\

CONFUSION: *"I'm curious about girls but not sexually aroused 100% of the time."*

REALITY: Healthy men are not obsessed with sex 100% of the time, or even most the time. An ongoing preoccupation with sexual arousal would be a warning sign of sexual addiction. When working through healing and recovery concepts, you should expect to have the preoccupation diminish over time. An expectation of trading obsessive thoughts about men for obsessive thoughts about women, is both unrealistic and unhealthy. Unbalanced constant preoccupation with sexual arousal is unhealthy. Objectification (treating a person as an object for one's personal pleasure) is neither healthy nor balanced. People are not objects. Healthy attraction toward the opposite sex should include emotional intimacy and connection. It should be peaceful but exciting.

\\

CONFUSION: *"I'm sensitive and emotional like a girl. Boys aren't supposed to be like that."*

REALITY: All boys experience emotion, but some cultures teach boys to hide their feelings. Some common messages in North American culture include: crying makes you a sissy, if you're afraid you're a wimp, or showing emotion makes you weak. These messages are just plain wrong. Some boys are more sensitive by disposition, but that doesn't mean they're weak or broken. It's okay to be sensitive. Other boys hide their emotions, but that doesn't mean they don't have feelings. Most boys and men show emotion when they can't contain it. Ever notice guys crying after a tough loss at an athletic event? Or when they jump on each other in excitement after winning a game? Start looking for examples of men expressing emotion. All men have feelings and can be sensitive and caring about one another.

\\

CONFUSION: *"I knew at a very young age that I was different."*

REALITY: Boys with attachment wounds typically feel different. Sometimes it's hard to pinpoint when those feelings started. They often describe feeling detached, connected more to girls, awkward around men, uncomfortable playing rough games, or other such descriptions. When you consider the emotional issues that accumulate from a very young age, it should be apparent as to why a young man might somehow believe he was always different. The attachment deficits and wounds we've discussed in this workbook occurred over the years beginning at a very early age. Learn to recognize the attachment issues that accumulated over time and work with a therapist on healing and recovery. The arousal patterns were years in the making and didn't happen overnight.

\\

Chapter 19 Questions

1. Go back and circle the "confusion" you can relate to. Why do you relate to the ones you circled? Explain each one.

_____

_____

_____

_____

_____

_____

_____

_____

_____

_____

_____

_____

2. When did the confusion arise? Write about a specific incident.

_____

_____

_____

_____

_____

_____

_____

_____

_____

_____

_____

_____

_____

_____

3. How does it help you to know you're similar to most boys? In other words, how does it feel to know that you're not so different?

_____

_____

_____

_____

_____

_____

_____

_____

_____

_____

4. Think about boys at school, your place of worship, or in your neighborhood. Can you think about times they might have been feeling the same as you?

_____

_____

_____

_____

_____

_____

_____

5. **ACTION ASSIGNMENT:** Perhaps someone you know had similar perceptions. Find someone you can interview and summarize their response.

_____

_____

_____

_____

_____

_____

_____

6. Write about any OTHER misperception or confusion you are realizing may have caused you to feel abnormal or different from other boys.

_____

_____

_____

_____

_____

_____

_____

_____

_____

_____

_____

_____

_____

_____

_____

_____

_____

_____

7. **ACTION ASSIGNMENT:** Find a trusted male mentor who is supporting you in recovery. Ask him about any misperceptions *he* had about *himself* growing up. When were times *he* felt abnormal or different? How did he go about changing those misperceptions? Now, write below what you learned.

_____

_____

_____

_____

_____

_____

_____

_____

_____

_____

_____

_____

_____

_____

_____

_____

Chapter 20

Launch Your Recovery

Unfortunately, harm has been done to those with sexualized attachments by well-intentioned people. On the extreme right, some have tried to "pray it away." This approach leaves individuals in a spiritual crisis when they don't experience magical cures.

On the extreme left, some have imposed labels and assume that everyone with same-sex urges must be gay. They ignore any possibility of emotional turmoil that might be at the root of confusion. Even left-leaning research has written about straight men with same-sex tendencies.[91] Frequently, youth with sexualized attachment issues have accepted labels they've been assigned.

Effective treatment should focus on healing attachment wounds, fulfilling attachment deficits, and addiction recovery (when this applies). You should focus on underlying issues. It's important that your view of recovery "success" is based on healing and recovery concepts.

Some religious leaders who preach obedience to God, but don't understand healing and recovery, are praying for magical cures. Similarly, some professional counselors may not have an education about sexualized attachment issues, and blindly place labels on their clients. Misguided focus in either direction can create frustration.

If you are reading this workbook because you want to change your attractions, then I would strongly encourage you to seek healing and recovery as your primary target. You must consistently apply principles of healing discussed in this book. Let go of your expectations about magical cures.

---

91 Ward, J. (2016). *Not Gay - Sex Between Straight White Men*. Paw Prints.

I interviewed a gentleman in recovery who told me the following story about his own life:

> "I didn't try to get help for a long time because I didn't think help was possible. I was sexually addicted and had a lot of emotional wounds. Sexual compulsions and severe depression became my lifestyle. I looked okay on the outside but was rotting away inside.
>
> I immersed myself in books, seminars, and counseling. I sorted through tons of information and began to understand the root causes of my struggles. I started to pinpoint the blocked fulfillment of legitimate needs. I felt unlovable, inadequate, insecure, and weak. So, I began working through past hurts.
>
> Most childhood experiences were not in my control, but they caused a distorted image of myself. Finding the true reasons for my confusion and depression gave me hope. I'm not just talking about behavior or surface stuff, I'm talking about deep down change."

For the purposes of this workbook, I have tried to depict the most common issues related to sexualized attachments. I've tried to explain concepts in a simple way. But you will need to become a detective in your self-discovery and apply principles for yourself. It may take some time, so be patient. Recovery is a marathon, not a sprint. It takes consistent, determined effort over time, not one quick burst of energy. Changes which occur because of solid recovery will take time. It took me several years. My friends in recovery share the same experience. Don't get discouraged... Just be persistent.

After attending my first men's conference, I walked away with a basic understanding of root issues. I was excited about the information because I had searched for so long. I had prayed to God for a cure, and later realized that God was not going to magically "cure" me. Rather, he wanted me to discover the wounds and deficits which might have been causing the turmoil; he wanted me to experience healing in my life. My confusion stemmed from legitimate human needs that God desired for me to satisfy, not ignore or pray away; needs for connection and attachment; needs for self-confidence and strength; needs for healing of emotional wounds. I started feeling change inside myself when these needs and wounds were resolved during recovery.

I heard a psychologist make a profound statement that resonated with me. She observed that some people with sexual confusion do not have abnormal needs, but that normal needs were left unmet or stunted as they were growing up. She said the needs as such were normal, but the lack of fulfillment, or barriers to fulfillment, was unhealthy and abnormal. Also, that healing implies the fulfillment of these unmet needs. She said that God does not cure people of legitimate needs.[92]

I like the way she said it, because it helps me to realize that all young men need to connect with one another. My attractions were often a reflection of legitimate needs; I wasn't inherently broken or different. She helped me feel normal.

My prayers in the past were blind. I was asking for something magical, rather than asking God to teach me. I learned that God wanted me to learn how to heal. He wanted me to find legitimate attachments and heal emotional wounds. When I started praying for God to open my eyes and give me courage, the answers were more apparent.[93] Doors began to open for healing opportunities.

Finding a Therapist

You probably won't be able to glean everything you need from this book alone. This workbook is meant as a beginning point. You will need to find other books and resources to assist you. I suggest you find a counselor who understands sexualized attachment issues. Once I found a counselor that was willing to learn, I met with him for over a year. That first year was pivotal in launching my progress.

Beware of counselors who seem to follow political agendas. Some are uneducated on the topic and cloud their judgment with political or personal opinions. You want a counselor who is open to learning and recognizing the various issues surrounding sexualized attachments in your life. Another friend in recovery told me: *"I not only struggled with sexuality, but I struggled equally to find professionals who understood my situation and how to help me heal. It was so difficult to explain myself to therapists who did not have a clue."*

In the process of finding a good counselor, you might consider asking some questions. Don't be afraid to call several different counselors and interview them over the phone. It will only take a few minutes. Listed below are some possible questions you might consider asking a counselor.

---

92 Moberly, E. R. (2006). Homosexuality: A New Christian Ethic. Lutterworth Press.

93 Joshua 1:9, NIV.

Possible Questions For A Counselor

1. Do you have an understanding of attachment theory?

2. Do you have any training about sexualized attachments?

3. What is your understanding of addiction recovery work?

4. Do you have an understanding of attachment wounds?

5. Tell me about your education and training in sexual addiction?

6. What therapeutic modalities do you use?

7. Have you done personal therapy in your own life?

Motivation

A committed motivation for healing and recovery is essential. You need a convicted desire to start this journey. Half-hearted efforts won't carry you through the process. Your desire must be strong enough that you'll do things you've never done. Your motivation must be stronger than your fear.

Constant temptation can be discouraging. I remember feeling engulfed by sexual preoccupation. The thoughts penetrated every moment of my day. I was like an alcoholic who never drinks, but constantly thinks about it.

I've talked to young men who start to experiment, and everything quickly morphed into compulsive sexual behavior. Innocent curiosity and exploration can turn into cycles of addiction. Sometimes temptation will cause you to vacillate and feel unsettled, but that's normal. If you are not committed, the temptation will be challenging and derail your efforts. If you don't have a burning desire and long-term commitment, then you won't succeed. Good recovery takes time, commitment, and persistence.

So, what can you do to strengthen your desire for healing and recovery? Start by referring often to this workbook and find additional resources that help maintain your goals. For example, motivating topics about success and goal-setting from famous public speakers or pastors can be helpful. You can also attend conferences where testimonials are given by those in recovery, listen to podcasts, review supportive websites, and listen to CDs, or watch DVDs. Parents, religious leaders, friends, or siblings who support your desire for healing can be a tremendous source of inspiration. Stay close to those people who want to encourage and support you. Find places where you can retreat to be uplifted, inspired, and encouraged to continue the journey. Again, remember this process is a marathon, not a sprint.

Establish Goals

If you want healing and recovery that stands the test of time, you will have goals to accomplish. Think of this process like a lawn covered with fallen leaves. You start raking in one spot, moving a few leaves at a time, until finally the yard is cleared of the fallen debris. Your recovery is a journey, not a one-time event. There will be times you'll work on several goals at the same time. At other times, you'll focus on one simple goal. Lasting recovery comes by making changes in your habits and lifestyle. You need to consider changing how you do life: Your source of encouragement, habits, routines, thoughts, and environment.

Realistic Expectations

I want you to have a realistic expectation about healing and recovery. There isn't a magical cure. Even when you're grounded and doing well, you'll need to do some maintenance throughout life. It's not much different than people who struggle with various other issues (e.g., alcoholism, anxiety, bulimia). These folks will also be working for maintenance in recovery with their respective issues.

For some of us, sexual confusion was a symptom that grew out of attachment needs and wounds over the lifespan. As a result, you might find an old thought or unwanted feeling pop into your mind. Perhaps during moments of distress your brain reverts to old patterns. One of my clients described an experience that's not uncommon:

> *"I've been happily married for several years with two young kids at home. But for some reason, when I lost my job the stress was intense. The rejection by my boss triggered memories of childhood abuse, and I found myself struggling again with old sexual thoughts from the past."*

It's not uncommon for this to happen. It doesn't mean you're not in recovery or that you haven't made changes. It means that your brain is defaulting to an old template. It may take several years for your brain to establish new patterns that feel more natural and automatic. Don't be discouraged by this normal occurrence, simply get back up and move forward.

Your brain might also default to its original template simply due to ongoing emotion. It doesn't have to be something dramatic like getting laid off at work. Just pick yourself up and keep going.

A teenage client said it this way:

"Sometimes I feel bored at home or just wish that I could spend more time with friends, and old feelings come back. It's almost like my need for adventure and connection reminds me of old stuff."

When I was fourteen, I memorized Beethoven's *Moonlight Sonata* and performed in competitions. I rehearsed the music for years. When I graduated from high school, I could still play most of the music without looking. Five years later, I could only play the first page from memory and the rest with the sheet music. Now over three decades later, I can only play it with the music in front of me. I can't remember anything from memory. Similarly, it may take some time to heal and forget emotional wounds.

I have a friend who has struggled with his weight. When he works hard through diet and exercise, he can lose the excess weight. But will he keep it off? That depends on his motivation to maintain new eating patterns and exercise habits. If he creates life-long recovery routines, the changes become more lasting.

However, it would not be uncommon for someone obese to have thoughts pop into his mind about delicious foods he previously could not resist. The brain may draw him back toward old patterns. If he reverts back, eventually he'll gain the weight back. But the longer he lives in new ways, the more lasting the weight-loss becomes. This is how recovery feels.

Beware of Pre-Addiction

Preoccupation may be only the tip of an iceberg. People with sexualized attachments are primed and ready for compulsive sexual activity. The emotional dynamics inside made us vulnerable to a more serious problem. The attachment issues were cultivating an emotional climate of addiction. These dynamics caused us to obsess and preoccupy. It fostered experimentation for some of my friends who soon found themselves swallowed up by addictive behavior beyond experimentation.

Be cautious if the confusion keeps you highly preoccupied. Approach your recovery as if you *could* become an addict. Don't ever put yourself in a situation to prove yourself. Don't test your sobriety-strength to see if you can abstain. Alcoholics Anonymous calls this a "slippery slope." In attempts to test yourself, you may find that old patterns rush over you. The emotional dynamics inside are primed for addiction potential, so be cautious.

I spoke to an enthusiastic young man who described his first arousal with a girlfriend. He wanted to see if the feelings were real. He wanted to test himself so he visited old porn sites to see what would happen. His brain quickly defaulted to the original template and previous memories returned. He found himself on a slippery slope. You cannot maintain new patterns when regularly returning to old ones.

Thoughts About God

I always thought I had been seeking God, but my prayers were often misdirected. I was asking God for magical cures. I was confused by sexual thoughts without realizing they were based on legitimate needs – longings for attachment that God had instilled within me; a desire to be loved by men, connected, accepted, and confident in the world of healthy masculinity. When I started praying for healing opportunities, God's response was more evident. God wanted me to feel loved, accepted, and affirmed.

If you are religious, you can pray for God to help you find buddies that will love you deeply; brothers with whom you can feel connected; mentors who will be affectionate; groups where you can find acceptance; and activities where you can develop confidence in your identity. Ask God where to find what you need. The Bible says: "Ask and it will be given to you; seek and you will find; knock and the door will be opened to you."[94]

Since God knows the details of your struggle, seek his assistance. He knows how to help you. You are his child, and He knows every hair on your head. He loves you as his creation more than anything else. He understands your pain. He asks us to seek Him. He wants to help you. Believe in a God that rescues. Trust Him to guide you for answers. He will lead you to the answers you need. It is my hope that you might find some of the answers within this book. Pray about these concepts to determine which ones are most pertinent to you. The Bible says: "The Lord is like a father to his children, tender and compassionate to those who fear him. For he knows how weak we are; he remembers we are only dust."[95]

Feeling unloved or rejected by family or peers is debilitating. If you feel abandoned or discarded by your earthly father, it may be hard to believe in a Heavenly Father who is faithfully committed to you; to believe in a God that has your best in mind. As a Christian, it gave me courage knowing that Christ died for me because he

---

94 Matthew 7:7, NIV.

95 Psalm 103:13, NLT.

DOES love me. "For God so loved the world [me] that He gave his one and only son, that whoever believes in him shall not perish but have eternal life."[96]

He wants you to know what it feels like to be loved by a father; that He cares for you so much He would give His own life to defend you. He wants to be there for you. He wants to fight for you. He wants to be your mentor and friend. He will go into battle with you. He won't leave you alone.

The Apostle Paul said, "No temptation has overtaken you except what is common to mankind. And God is faithful; he will not let you be tempted beyond what you can bear. But when you are tempted, he will also *provide a way out* so that you can endure it."[97] Notice that Paul says God prepares *a way out*. In other words, God knows that sometimes temptation will be overwhelming, and He provides a way out so you can escape.

Remember that God is watching. He's your greatest fan. He's happy you're finding answers. This is what God means when John says, "Then you will know the truth, and the truth will set you free."[98]

After you finish this book go back and decide which areas need your attention and effort. When I first started recovery, I realized that my relationship with male peers was most damaged, so that is where my goals and healing started. After reading this book and doing some introspection, you will have a better idea of where you need to begin. Seek the advice of a professional counselor. Set goals and create a plan of action. Share these goals with supportive family, friends, and mentors. You can do this.

---

96 John 3:16, NIV.

97 1Cor 10:13, NIV.

98 John 8:32, NIV.

Chapter 20 Questions

1. What other concerns or questions do you have about recovery?

_____

_____

_____

_____

_____

_____

_____

_____

_____

2. Do you know someone who has been harmed by a bad therapist? Discuss this with your therapist.

_____

_____

_____

_____

_____

_____

_____

3. What insights have you gleaned from this workbook?

_____

_____

_____

_____

_____

_____

_____

_____

_____

_____

_____

4. Have you ever been discouraged because people labeled you without understanding you?

_____

_____

_____

_____

_____

_____

_____

_____

5. You'll need to find a therapist who understands sexualized attachment issues and recovery concepts. What do you want to make sure your counselor understands about you and your story?

_____

_____

_____

_____

_____

_____

_____

_____

_____

6. Can you identify some of the goals you need to set?

_____

_____

_____

_____

_____

_____

_____

7. On a scale of one to ten, how strong is your motivation for healing and recovery? Circle the number.

1   2   3   4   5   6   7   8   9   1 0

8. Explain why you circled that number and discuss with your counselor:

_____

_____

_____

_____

_____

_____

_____

_____

9. What does it mean to maintain recovery? Discuss with your mentor and counselor.

_____

_____

_____

_____

_____

_____

_____

_____

_____

10. Have you felt as though you might be in a pre-addiction state? What types of thoughts or behaviors lead you to this conclusion?

_____

_____

_____

_____

_____

_____

11. Why does a pre-addiction state make experimentation dangerous?

_____

_____

_____

_____

_____

_____

12. How could you start making prayer more effective for yourself?

_____

_____

_____

_____

_____

_____

13. **ACTION ASSIGNMENT:** Find an adult that you can trust and talk with him/
her about religious and spiritual issues that relate to your healing and recovery.
Write down what you learned in the discussion.

_____

_____

_____

_____

_____

_____

14. What holds you back from healing and recovery?

_____

_____

_____

_____

_____

_____

15. List the resources you've explored thus far to find answers.

_____

_____

_____

_____

_____

Chapter 21

Recovery Tools

There's a lot to accomplish in the process of healing and recovery, so try to avoid discouragement. Take one goal at a time and recognize forward movement. Use the tools in this chapter to help you along.

Make your recovery a team sport and you'll be more successful. Share the tools with your mentors and counselor. Create a team that surrounds you with support. It helps when others know your goals. When you share, you'll generate opportunities with someone to unconditionally accept and support you.[99] Men work together in a team to win games and fight battles. They support each other in the arena and on the battlefield. Develop your team.

Plan of Action

Below is an example of a "Plan of Action." You might choose to add or eliminate items to fit your individual situation. Review your plan monthly and adjust as needed.

Date: *January*

My Bottom Lines (Behaviors I need to stop)

I will not watch pornography.

My Self Esteem Box (This is a box you create to help remind yourself of all your positive qualities.)

I will complete my box by (date): *January 20*

People I can call when I need to talk or I'm lonely:

Uncle Tyler, Logan, Grandpa, Nathan

EXAMPLE

---

99 Baer, G. (2003). *Real love: The truth about finding unconditional love and fulfilling relationships*. New York: Gotham Books, p. 47.

Meetings

Individual counseling: *Meet with Jason weekly*

Support group meetings: *Attend SA weekly*

Visit with pastor: *Monthly visit with pastor John*

Youth group/religious: *Attend weekly small group; try to open up.*

Visit with a mentor: *Uncle Tyler*

Personal Reflection

Recovery reading material (15 minutes daily):

Healing & Recovery daily, search for other helpful materials

Journaling:

Start journaling every day the things in the workbook that apply to me, and how I'm doing on the healing concepts.

Spirituality

Prayer:

Every evening and morning, pause to think when I pray.

Scripture study:

Bible reading plan - 10 mins/day.

Service to others:

Volunteer to help with skateboard ministry or basketball ministry for neighborhood kids on Mon/Wed afternoons.

Body

Ways I can get healthy touch and affection:

Ask uncle Tyler for a hug when I see him, try to greet some of my friends with a hug or knuckles.

Plan for getting enough sleep (you'll have more difficulties when tired):

Bedtime 10:30pm

Plan for eating healthy (you'll have more difficulties if malnourished):

Eat all three meals and bring granola bars in backpack for afternoon during gym.

Physical Exercise:

Morning run before classes

Bonding

Adult mentors I look up to and who could spend time with me:

Uncle Tyler, pastor John, grandpa, maybe coach Richard after practice.

Activities I can do with mentors:

I want grandpa to teach me how to fish, uncle Tyler said he'd help me learn basketball, pastor John take me for ice cream.

Young men I would like to develop a connection with:

Noah and Aaron from school, Layton from small group, my cousins Willum and Jeffrey.

Activities I can do with other young men:

My cousins like to play pickup ball at the park, go to movie, hang out after school, online video games.

Healthy Masculinity

Activities I can learn which would help me feel confident:

Ask uncle Tyler to help me learn basketball, I really want to learn how to play without anxiety.

Talents I can develop which would help me feel confident:

Basketball, learning how to socialize better with guys at school.

I'd also like to ask a girl to prom.

Other:

I'd like to change my clothes - my "look." Need to ask my

cousins for advice on this.

My Plan of Action

Date: _____

My Bottom Lines (Behaviors I need to stop)

_____

_____

_____

_____

_____

_____

_____

_____

My Self Esteem Box (This is a box you create to help remind yourself of all your positive qualities.)

I will complete my box by (date): _____

People I can call when I need to talk or I'm lonely:

_____

_____

_____

_____

_____

_____

_____

Meetings

Individual counseling: _____

Support group meetings: _____

Visit with pastor: _____

Youth group/religious: _____

Visit with a mentor: _____

Personal Reflection

Recovery reading material (15 minutes daily):

_____

_____

_____

_____

_____

Journaling:

_____

_____

_____

_____

_____

_____

_____

Spirituality

Prayer:

_____

_____

_____

_____

_____

_____

Scripture study:

_____

_____

_____

_____

_____

Service to others:

_____

_____

_____

_____

Body

Ways I can get healthy touch and affection:

_____

_____

_____

_____

_____

_____

Plan for getting enough sleep (you'll have more difficulties when tired):

_____

_____

_____

Plan for eating healthy (you'll have more difficulties if malnourished):

_____

_____

_____

_____

Physical Exercise:

_____

_____

_____

_____

Bonding

Adult mentors I look up to and who could spend time with me:

_____

_____

_____

_____

_____

Activities I can do with mentors:

_____

_____

_____

_____

_____

_____

Young men I would like to develop a connection with:

_____

_____

_____

_____

_____

_____

Activities I can do with other young men:

_____

_____

_____

_____

_____

Healthy Masculinity

Activities I can learn which would help me feel confident:

_____

_____

_____

_____

_____

Talents I can develop which would help me feel confident:

_____

_____

_____

_____

_____

Other:

_____

_____

_____

_____

_____

_____

_____

_____

_____

_____

_____

_____

_____

_____

_____

_____

Check-In

Find adults and friends with whom you can check-in. I suggest checking in regarding four areas of healing: Buddies, Mentors, Masculinity, and Body. Below is a chart for checking in that you can use to remember. There is an example and a blank one you can copy.

Check-In
"Four Areas of Healing"

EXAMPLE

MENTORS	BUDDIES
(Relationship with an older or wiser man who can help guide you)	(Relationship with male peers who help you integrate a sense of belonging - "one of the guys")
• Asked my dad if he would help me learn to fish. • Pastor at church spent time talking with me about my struggles. • Met with my older brother and told him I needed his help.	• Hung out with new friends during Superbowl game. • Asked guy from school to play golf. • Went camping with buddies.
HEALTHY MASCULINITY	**BODY**
(Grounding yourself in healthy masculinity)	(Issues such as affection, body shame, emotional expression, curiosity)
• Signed up for softball clinic. • Went with dad to batting cages. • Started going to gym with mentor. • Went to the locker room to change for PE instead of avoiding it. • Attended a basketball game.	• Asked my dad to hug me. • Practiced knuckles with buddies. • Gave hugs to buddies after hangout. • Went on campout and went swimming with everyone. • Allowed myself to cry in front of my uncle.

Check-In
"Four Areas of Healing"

MENTORS	BUDDIES
(Relationship with an older or wiser man who can help guide you)	*(Relationship with male peers who help you integrate a sense of belonging - "one of the guys")*

HEALTHY MASCULINITY	BODY
(Grounding yourself in healthy masculinity)	*(Issues such as affection, body shame, emotional expression, curiosity)*

The Barometer

The "Barometer" is a tool similar to a weather barometer. When the atmospheric pressure goes up you know it's going to rain. Similarly, when the emotional pressure goes up, sexual preoccupation often goes up. When attachment needs are satisfied in healthy ways, emotional issues are addressed and other wounds resolved, the pressure goes down and sexual preoccupation is usually reduced.

Use the barometer tool below to help analyze events that might be making preoccupation more intense.

- Circle the number that represents the strength of your preoccupation (one is weak and ten is strongest).

- Think back over the recent past and determine if there were events that transpired which opened old wounds, or left you with emotional conflict or distress.

- List these events on the right side of the page under "Issues that raise preoccupation."

- Finally, at the bottom list things you can do to satisfy needs for connection and resolve emotional distress. These are things that reduce emotional pressure.

The example on the next page will illustrate. Take your time. You may want to periodically fill out a barometer worksheet and review it with a mentor or counselor.

The Barometer

	ISSUES THAT RAISE PREOCCUPATION
10	
9	
8	Kept comparing myself at school to other guys.
7	Felt really loney - parents told me to figure it out on my own.
6	I felt jealous during PE watching the guys play basketball.
5	I watched football players eat lunch together and envied their friendship.
4	I felt inferior in the locker room because in I don't have big muscles.
3	Guys made fun of me at school.
2	I got super angry at my dad and couldn't stop thinking about it.
1	Dad told me that I was stupid.

(left axis, top to bottom: Strong Preoccupation → Low Preoccupation)

EXAMPLE

Plan to reduce the pressure:

I'm going to spend some time with my uncle and talk — he listens. Will try and plan a fishing trip with new friend Andrew — he offered to teach me — I've always wanted to learn. Going to call another friend and go to the gym to feel included. Will respond to the youth group's invitation to go to the movies on Friday — be part of the group. Will ask for a hug from Tait.

The Barometer

	ISSUES THAT RAISE PREOCCUPATION
10	
9	
8	
7	
6	
5	
4	
3	
2	
1	

Strong Preoccupation

Low Preoccupation

Plan to reduce the pressure:

_____

_____

_____

_____

_____

A.I.M.

Sometimes a specific situation or person causes specific thoughts or feelings. Perhaps these situations or people trigger the preoccupation. The AIM tool can help you to decipher the emotional undercurrent and pressure that generates the trigger.

A - Acknowledge:

There is almost always a message underneath the preoccupation. God is communicating to you something important. Take a moment to acknowledge some deeper message inside you.

I - Identify:

What is the message underneath the preoccupation? The preoccupation teaches you about emotions, needs, and wounds. Could it be that you look at some other guy and feel envy because of the way he looks? Could it be that you feel jealous watching other men play sports or do athletic things? Could it be that you feel deeply alone when you watch boys banter with one another?

M - Move:

Once you've identified the message, you must move into action. If it was envy, find creative solutions to resolve that envy. Perhaps it was jealousy about other young men's athleticism, so identify goals to resolve the jealousy. If it was about loneliness, you might have to develop friendships with buddies and mentors. If you don't move into the messages, the preoccupation does not diminish.

A.I.M.

Fill out this worksheet as often as needed until you are good at doing it in your head.

A	**(ACKNOWLEDGE)** Say something to acknowledge the message: *My preoccupation is really strong right now watching a dad at church putting his arm around his teenage son.* EXAMPLE
I	**(IDENTIFY)** What was the message? *My father-hunger has never gone away. I'm still really starved to have a adult figure in my life who cares about me and wants to be there for me. This preoccupation is based on my unmet need for a father-figure.*
M	**(MOVE)** How can you move into the message? *I'm going to call my uncle Steve and ask if he'll spend some time with me. I'm going to get more honest with him about how hard it has been not having a father-figure to be there for me. I might even ask him for a hug.*

HEALING & RECOVERY

A	**(ACKNOWLEDGE)** Say something to acknowledge the message:
I	**(IDENTIFY)** What was the message?
M	**(MOVE)** How can you move into the message?

Notes

Notes

About the Author

Floyd Godfrey received a PhD in Clinical Sexology and is a Licensed Professional Counselor. He is a Certified Sex Addiction Therapist (CSAT) and a Certified Clinical Sexologist (CCS). He received his education from the International Institute of Clinical Sexology, Arizona State University, and from Ottawa University. He worked for eight years with Tempe Social Services as a supervisor assisting school-age children and their families.

Floyd is the founder of the HOPE Mental Health Foundation, a non-profit organization that provides financial support and programming to those who need mental health services. He also serves on the board of education for Canyon State Academy, a residential school setting for at-risk youth. He is the Director of the Sexual Addiction & Betrayal Trauma Recovery program (SABR), a clinical intervention for men with sexual addiction and their partners. He also facilitates the Band of Brothers program, which is a clinical intervention for adolescent boys with sexual compulsions. He is a member of SASH (Society for the Advancement of Sexual Health) and the AACC (American Association of Christian Counselors). He currently serves as the Executive Director of Family Strategies Counseling Center, where he trains and supervises clinical staff and university interns. He works part-time within the agency to provide individual counseling for adults, youth, and families.

Floyd has been married to his bride, Kaleen, for thirty years, and together they've raised three wonderful children. While he is committed to clinical excellence, Floyd maintains a personal worldview of Biblical living and believes that faith in God is important for spiritual healing. He recognizes his need for a Savior and has accepted Jesus Christ into his life.

Bibliography

Baer, G. (2003). *Real love: The truth about finding unconditional love and fulfilling relationships.* New York: Gotham Books.

Bailey, J. M., & Pillard, R. C. (1991). A Genetic Study of Male Sexual Orientation. *Archives of General Psychiatry, 48*(12), 1089.

Baron, M. (1993). Genetic linkage and male homosexual orientation. *Bmj,307*(6900).

Benedict, F. (2017). *Life After Lust - Stories & Strategies for Sex & Pornography Addiction Recovery.* Visionary Books.

Benjamin, B. & Werner R. (n.d.). *The Primacy of Human Touch*, HEALTH Newsletter. http://www.benbenjamin.com/articles.html.

Bothe, B., Toth-Kieraly, I., Potenza, M., Gabor, O., & Demetrovics, Z. (2020). High-Frequency Pornography Use May Not Always Be Problematic. *The Journal of Sexual Medicine*, 1–20. https://doi.org/10.1016/j.jsxm.2020.01.007

Breaux, M. (n.d.). Retrieved from http://www.drmonicabreaux.com.

Brotherson, L. (n.d.). StrengtheningMarriage.com. Retrieved July 28, 2018, from https://www.strengtheningmarriage.com.

Carnes, P., & Carnes, P. (2001). *Out of the shadows: Understanding sexual addiction.* Center City, MN: Hazelden Information & Edu.

Carnes, P. (1994). *Contrary to love: Helping the sexual addict.* Center City, MN: Hazelden Foundation.

Cooper, Delmonico, and Burg, "Cybersex Users, Abusers, and Compulsives: New Findings and Implications," *Sexual Addiction and Compulsivity: The Journal of Treatment and Prevention 7*, nos. 1-2 (2000), as cited by Carnes, P., & Carnes, P. (2001). Out of the shadows.

Crawford, D. (1998). *Easing the Ache: Gay men recovering from compulsive behaviors.* Center City, Minn: Hazelden.

Diamond, L. M. (2009). *Sexual fluidity: Understanding women's love and desire.* Cambridge, MA: Harvard University Press.

Dobson, J. C. (2005). *Bringing up boys.* Carol Stream, IL: Tyndale House.

Dusek, D. (2015). *Rough Cut Men - A Man's Battle Guide to Building Real Relationships with Each Other and with Jesus.* Issaquah, WA: Made For Success Publishing.

Ethridge, S. (2012). *The Fantasy fallacy: Exposing the deeper meaning behind sexual thoughts.* Waterville, Me.: Christian Large Print Originals.

Fawcett, D. (2018, May). *Chemsex, Sex Addiction and Men Who have Sex with Men: Effective Strategies.* Speaker presentation of the IITAP Symposium, Scottsdale, AZ.

Fitzgibbons, R., MD. (n.d.). Library: The Origins and Healing of Homosexual Attractions. Retrieved July 28, 2018, from https://www.catholicculture.org/culture/library/view.cfm?id=3112.

Flores, P. J. (2012). *Addiction as an attachment disorder.* Lanham: Jason Aronson.

Greene, M. (2017, August 07). Touch Isolation: How Homophobia Has Robbed All Men of Touch. Retrieved from https://medium.com/@remakingmanhood/touch-isolation-how-homophobia-has-robbed-all-men-of-touch-239987952f16.

Grubbs, J., & Gola, M. (2019). Is Pornography Use Related to Erectile Functioning? Results From Cross-Sectional and Latent Growth Curve Analyses. *The Journal of Sexual Medicine, 16*(1), 111–125. https://doi.org/https://doi.org/10.1016/j.jsxm.2018.11.004

Grubbs, J. B., Carlisle, R., Hook, J., Pargament, K., & Exline, J. J. (2015, January). *Transgression as addiction: religiosity and moral disapproval as predictors of perceived addiction to pornography.* Archives of sexual behavior. https://pubmed.ncbi.nlm.nih.gov/24519108/.

Gurian, M. (2006). *The wonder of boys: What parents, mentors and educators to do to shape boys into exceptional men.* New York: Jeremy P. Tarcher/Penguin.

Hilton, D. (2012, July). *Pornography & Addiction: Neuroscience Considerations.* Speaker presentation of the LifeSTAR Conference 2012, Salt Lake City, UT.

Hilton, D. (2018, July). *The Sex Industry and Public Health: It's Impact on Exploitation, Healthy Sexuality, Empathy and Addiction.* Speaker presentation of the LifeSTAR Annual Conference 2018, Salt Lake City, UT.

Hunt, J. (Director). (2017). *Absent - One Man Makes a World of Difference*[Video file]. USA: Time & Tide Productions. Retrieved from www.absentmovie.com. A film addressing the wounds left by an absent father.

Journal of Human Sexuality,1(1). (2009).

Jones, S. L., & Yarhouse, M. A. (2007). *Ex-gays?: A longitudinal study of religiously mediated change in sexual orientation.* Downers Grove, IL: IVP Academic.

Karges, C. (2016, August 23). Attachment Issues & Sexuality. Retrieved July 27, 2018, from https://www.addictionhope.com/blog/attachment-issues-sexuality.

Kastleman, M. B. (2001). *The drug of the new millennium: The science of how internet pornography radically alters the human brain and body. Orem, UT: Granite Pub.*

Katehakis, A. (2010). *Erotic intelligence: Igniting hot, healthy sex while in recovery from sex addiction.* Deerfield Beach, FL: Health Communications.

Katehakis, A. (2016). *Sex addiction as affect dysregulation: A neurobiologically informed holistic treatment.* New York: W. W. Norton & company.

King, N. (2000). Childhood Sexual Trauma in Gay Men. *Journal of Gay & Lesbian Social Services,12*(1-2), 19-35.

Kirk, M., & Madsen, H. (1990). *After the ball: How America will conquer its fear and hatred of gays in the 90s.* New York: Plume.

Kort, J., & Morgan, A. P. (2014). *Is my husband gay, straight, or bi?: A guide for women concerned about their men.* Lanham: Rowman & Littlefield.

Levay, S. (1991). A difference in hypothalamic structure between heterosexual and homosexual men. *Science,253*(5023), 1034-1037.

Love, T. L. (2017). *Finding Peace - A Workbook on Healing from Loss, Neglect, Rejection, Abandonment, Betrayal and Abuse.* Yuma, AZ: Love and Light Publishing.

''Luca era gay" by Povia & Monia Russo (with English subtitles) Official music video. (2009, May 02). Retrieved from https://youtu.be/583GBge-U-c.

Marshall, E. (1995, June 30). NIHs "gay gene" study questioned. *Science*.

Martinez, L. (2017, February 10). *Professor strikes down 'born this way' argument for homosexuality.* Retrieved from https://badgerherald.com/news/2017/02/10/professor-strikes-down-born-this-way-argument-for-homosexuality.

McKay, B & McKay K., *"Bosom Buddies: A Photo History of Male Affection,"* (http://artofmanliness.com).

Moberly, E. R. (2006). *Homosexuality: A New Christian Ethic.* Lutterworth Press

Molitor, B. D. (2001). *A Boy's Passage - Celebrating Your Son's Journey to Maturity.* Colorado Springs, CO: WaterBrook Press.

Mooney, C. G. (2010). *Theories of attachment: An introduction to Bowlby, Ainsworth, Gerber, Brazelton, Kennell, and Klaus.* St. Paul, MN: Redleaf Press.

"Neurosurgeon Dr. Donald Hilton Reveals Shocking Scientific Truths About Porn." (n.d.). Video retrieved from https://fightthenewdrug.org/media/neurosurgeon-donald-hilton-jr-truths-about-porn-harms-brain.

Pollack, W. S. (1999). *Real boys: Rescuing our sons from the myths of boyhood.* New York: Henry Holt and Company.

Regenerus, M. (2012). *How Different Are the Adult Children of Parents Who Have Same-Sex Relationships? Findings from the New Family Structures Study.* Social Science Research, Vol. 41, No. 4 (June 2012), pp. 752–770.

Robinson, J., Dr. (n.d.). Understanding Unwanted Same-Sex Attraction. Retrieved August 10, 2018, from http://www.theguardrail.com/

Ryan, T. C. (2012). *Ashamed No More: A Pastors Journey Through Sex Addiction.* InterVarsity Press.

Saranthaos, S. (1996). Children Australia. *Children Australia,21,* 23.

Sex Addicts Anonymous. (2017). Houston, TX: International Service Organization SAA.

Schumm, W. R. (2010). Children of Homosexuals More Apt to Be Homosexuals? A Reply to Morrison And to Cameron Based on an Examination of Multiple Sources of Data. *Journal of Biosocial Science,42*(06).

Savin-Williams, R. C. (2017). *Mostly straight: Sexual fluidity among men.* Cambridge, MA: Harvard University Press.

Sexual Orientation and Homosexuality, (n.d.). Retrieved July 28, 2018, from http://www.apa.org/topics/lgbt/orientation.aspx

Spitzer, R. (2003). *Archives of Sexual Behavior, Vol. 32, No. 5, Oct 2003*, pp. 403-417.

Time Magazine, (1998, April 27).

Timms, R. J., & Connors, P. (1999). *Embodying healing: Integrating bodywork and psychotherapy in recovery from childhood sexual abuse.* Brandon, VT: Safer Society Press.

Van, B. A. (1989, June). The compulsion to repeat the trauma. Re-enactment, revictimization, and masochism. Retrieved from https://www.ncbi.nlm.nih.gov/pubmed/2664732

Ward, J. (2016). *Not Gay - Sex Between Straight White Men.* Paw Prints.

Weiss, R., & Schneider, J. P. (2015). *Always turned on: Sex addiction in the digital age.* Carefree, AZ: Gentle Path Press.

Weiss, R. (2015). *Sex addiction 101: A basic guide to healing from sex, porn, and love addiction.* Deerfield Beach, FL: Health Communications.

What About Therapy for Our Same-Sex Attractions? (2012). Retrieved July 28, 2018, from http://www.brothersroad.org/therapy. Survey of men with incongruous homosexual attractions who sought treatment.

Whitehead, N., & Whitehead, B. (2015). *My genes made me do it: Homosexuality and the scientific evidence.* United States: Whitehead Associates.

Wilson, G. (2017). *Your brain on porn: Internet pornography and the emerging science of addiction.* Margate, Kent, United Kingdom: Commonwealth Publishing.

Wright, L. B., & Loiselle, M. B. (1997). *Back on track: Boys dealing with sexual abuse.* Brandon: Safer Society Press.

"Adversity toughens manhood, and the characteristic of the good or the great man is not that he has been exempt from the evils of life, but that he has surmounted them."

–Patrick Henry

www.ingramcontent.com/pod-product-compliance
Lightning Source LLC
Chambersburg PA
CBHW080249030426
42334CB00023BA/2750

9 780578 904825